DELUSIONS OF BRANDEUR

BY RYAN WALLMAN

A *...Gasp!* **BOOK**

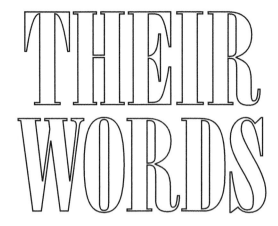

THEIR WORDS

"Wallman slips into his Raging Bull costume and stampedes through the marketing industry smashing every bit of phony china in sight. What wonderful fun!"
Bob Hoffman, Author, Former Advertising CEO, and the original Ad Contrarian.

"Marketing leaders the world over, get your hands on this book. You may not have mine because I can't put it down (except when weeping with laughter)."
Maureen Blandford, B2B Tech CMO, Author.

"I love this book. Anything I spend my time on, I either have to learn something or be entertained, with this book I get both - along with great art direction. The only problem is that the people it takes the piss out of won't know how funny it is. But that's okay, they'll buy it thinking it's a genuine 'How to' guide."
Dave Trott, Author and Advertising Legend.

"Marketing has been walking around in the emperor's new clothes, with a big pair of shiny new AI/VR bollocks on public display, but Ryan has thankfully come along and lopped them off with his sharp satirical scythe of perceptive brilliance."
Giles Edwards, Co-Founder and Creative Director at Gasp.

"As with all really good satire, smuggled inside every one of Wallman's lovingly-crafted jokes is a serious message: that too many marketers reject proven principles for unproven pseudo-science, plain English for pretentious marketing jargon, the tried and tested for the shiny and new."
Tom Roach, Head of Effectiveness at adam&eveDDB.

"A former doctor takes a scalpel to the advertising industry. Not only is this a marvellous book - but no one but Dr. Wallman could have written it."
Rory Sutherland, Vice Chairman at Ogilvy UK, TED Global speaker, Author.

"Is it a guide book for our industry? Or is it a good laugh at our industry? It's both. It's Ryan at his most erudite and entertaining. And it's Gasp at their most gorgeous. Get it to get ahead - or to get the hell out of the mess we've made of marketing, branding and advertising."
Vikki Ross, Copy Chief.

"Thoroughly digestible, very insightful, loads of great tips (for people who are trapped in places where the bullshit is inescapable) and funny as fuck – cutting through the nonsense in the way that only Ryan knows how. Top work."
Dave Harland, Copywriter.

"The good Doctor slides his satirical blade between the Marketing body's ribs using humour as laughing gas. Just wait 'til they all come round. And it's not as funny as they thought."
Mark Sareff, Director at Prophecy Consulting & former Chief Strategy Officer at Ogilvy Australia.

"Marketing as we know it is dead. It's just been completely annihilated by Ryan Wallman. Somewhere between a comedy roast and a how-not-to guide, this book is an utter goldmine for the beginners, side-splitting for the seasoned, and utterly baffling for the 'experts'. Satire so sharp it will slice you – and you'll say thank you."
Clare Barry, Copywriter and Queen of Sass.

"Any book that references Derek and Clive gets my vote, and so should it yours. But even without that, the vitriolic attack Ryan has mounted on all things advertising is wonderful. I'd say it was funny, if it weren't so sadly accurate and well-observed. A damning indictment that'll make you laugh, cry and shut down your LinkedIn account at the earliest opportunity. Buy it. And then pray to Ogilvy you don't recognise too much of yourself"
Glenn Fisher, Author, The Art of the Click.

...*Gasp!*
22 Market Place
Wokingham
Berkshire
RG40 1AP
GREAT BRITAIN

Tel: +44 (0)118 9797000
Web: Gasp.Agency

First published in 2019
Copyright ©Ryan Wallman & Gasp Four Ltd.

The right of Ryan Wallman to be identified as the Author has been
asserted in accordance with the Copyright, Design and Patents Act 1988.

DELUSIONS OF BRANDEUR

BY RYAN WALLMAN

A ...*Gasp!* **BOOK**

ABOUT THE AUTHOR

Ryan Wallman is Creative Director and Head of Copy at Wellmark, a Melbourne-based creative agency that specialises in healthcare. In his former life, he was a doctor and worked for several years in psychiatry – so he knows plenty about delusions.

Ryan is an internationally acclaimed copywriter and marketing commentator. He has written for numerous industry publications, including Marketing Week, the Australian Financial Review and The Economic Times. He is also a co-author of the bestselling book 'Eat Your Greens: Fact-Based Thinking to Improve Your Brand's Health'.

Something of a contrarian, Ryan is known for his no-nonsense approach to marketing, and has twice been listed in Business Insider's 'Best 30 People in Advertising to Follow on Twitter'.

Along with his medical degree, Ryan has a Master of Marketing from Melbourne Business School and a Graduate Certificate in Professional Writing. He has vowed to never study again.

MESSAGE FROM THE AUTHOR

Hello!

And welcome.

If you work in marketing, you'll know very well that the world doesn't need another marketing book. But I've written one anyway.

Well, sort of – this isn't really a marketing book in the conventional sense. Hell, it's not even a book in the conventional sense.

It's a collection of articles, satirical posts and assorted miscellany that I've written over the past few years. In fact, if you follow me on Twitter, you've probably seen most of it already. Sorry about that.

While this book is largely lighthearted, I like to think there is a serious message behind the humour. Many of us roll our eyes at the unsubstantiated claims made by the, ahem, louder voices in our industry, but plenty of others take them as gospel. And that's a huge problem for marketers and the businesses they serve.

Therefore, I hope there is enough in here to make you laugh *and* think (a bit).

So, thanks very much for buying it. Unless you've borrowed it from someone, of course – in which case, thanks for nothing. (Just kidding. I probably wouldn't pay for it either.)

MESSAGE FROM GASP

If this book was written 11 years ago, just before Gasp started, it could easily have been the founding satirical tome of all that we stand for.

But it wasn't.

It was written very much in the present, and comes to print at a time when it is very much needed; to cut through the jargon in an industry that is a minefield of utter boll*cks and is replete with charlatans looking to sell shiny new bottles of snake oil.

It makes us both proud and excited (not to say a little envious of Ryan's writing prowess) to have designed and published Delusions of Brandeur. We would be lying if we said we were not a little daunted at the start of the process: how do you make the book look artistically as good and as sharp as it reads? What a challenge. And it's our first ever book to boot.

The final piece, we'd humbly like to think, goes a good way to achieving that, with Ryan's talent making our job easier by providing us with huge inspiration.

So please read on, and we hope you enjoy reading it half as much as we enjoyed designing it.

Giles Edwards.

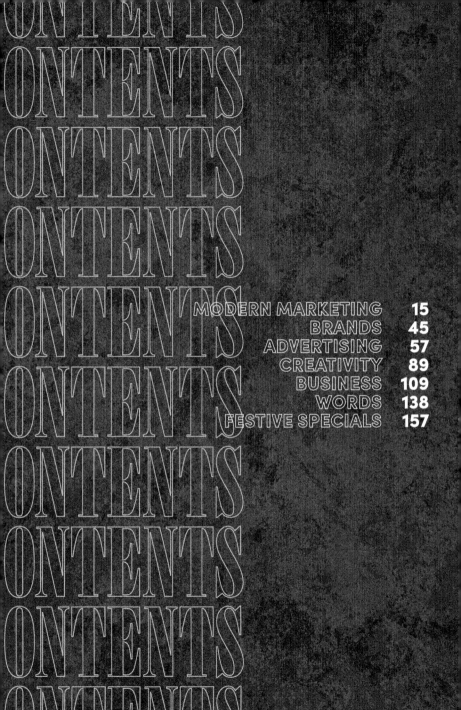

CHAPTER

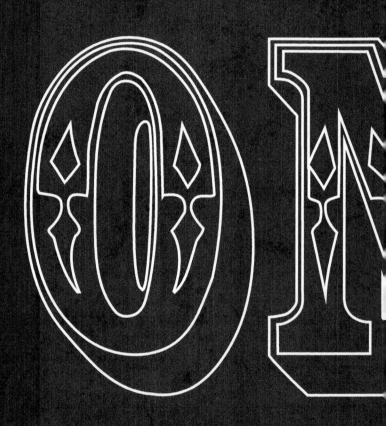

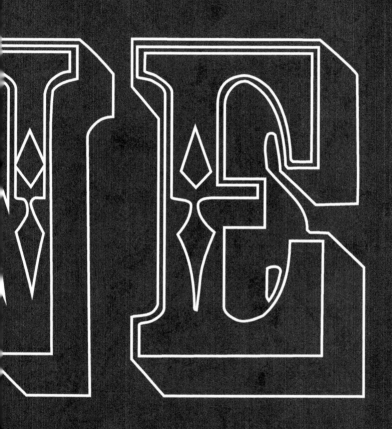

MODERN MARKETING

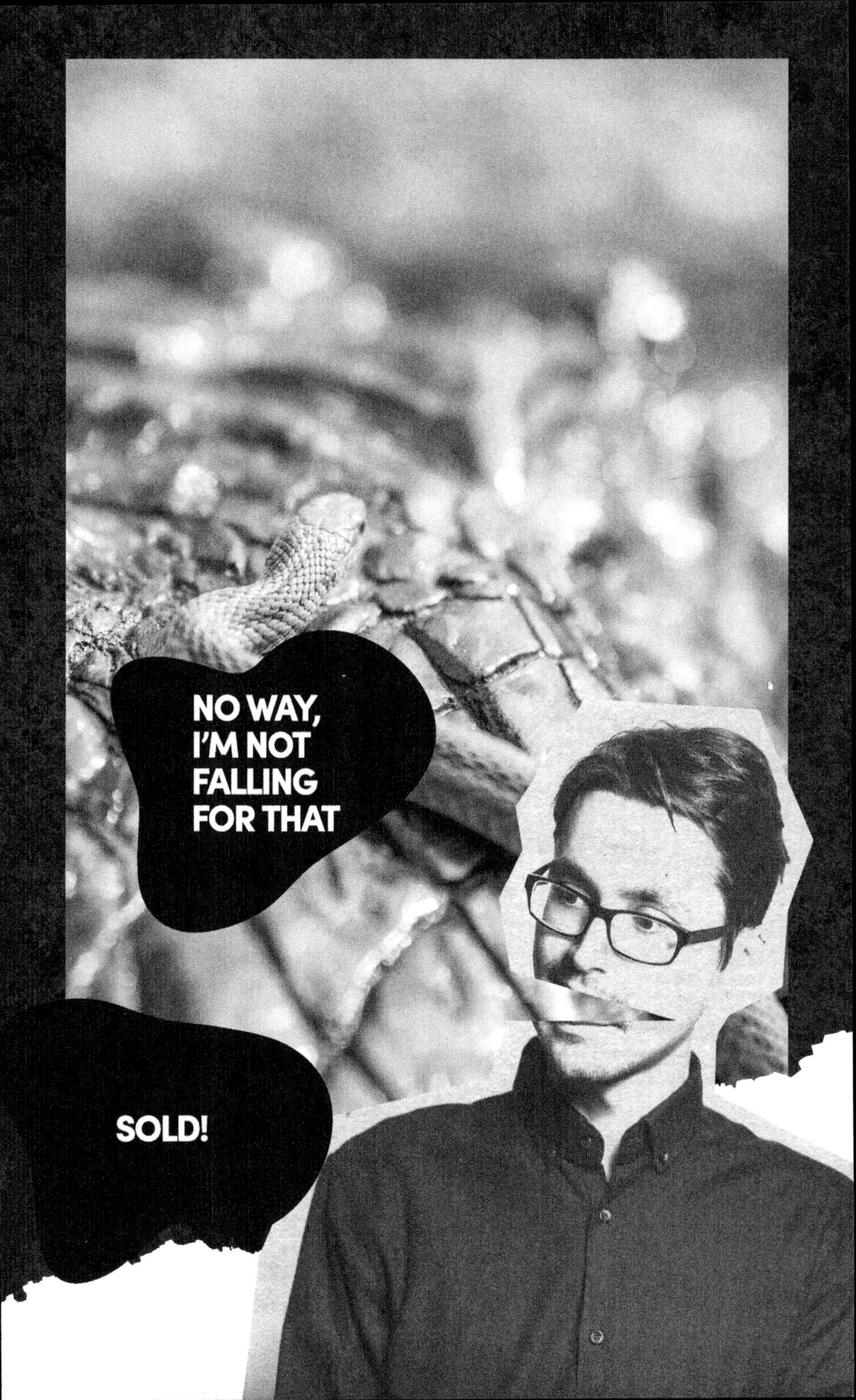
NO WAY, I'M NOT FALLING FOR THAT
SOLD!

THE LAWS

THE LAWS

THE LAWS

THE LAWS

THE LAWS OF MODERN MARKETING

Choose digital first, ask questions later.

The target market is millennials. Always.

When everybody else zigs, you must zig too. Jumping on the latest fad is a foolproof way to achieve long-term growth.

Talking is the new thinking.

A 3-millisecond view by an online bot is a more reliable measure of reach than half an hour of TV viewing by a human.

The best way to understand your customers is to extrapolate from your own experiences.

Education is for losers.

There is no business problem that can't be solved by a gimmicky app and a massive dose of hubris.

When in doubt, misrepresent the data.

Marketers over the age of 30 know nothing. And they smell funny.

THE DIGITAL DELUSION IN MARKETING

The chief marketing officer of Pepsi Co North America Beverages was recently quoted as saying:

"Consumers' attention spans have changed, and no one is watching television without using a device at the same time."

Leaving aside the almost certainly false claim that consumers' attention spans have changed, I found his assertion that no one is watching television without using a device at the same time to be the most worrying part of this statement.

Clearly, he uses a device (a phone, presumably) when he watches TV. Equally clearly, the people he knows also use a device when they watch TV. But to suggest that no one does otherwise betrays a staggering ignorance for a senior marketer.

And he's not alone, either. The 2016 UK Ad Nation study, conducted by Ipsos Connect and commissioned by Thinkbox, found that marketers estimated the proportion of people multi-screening while watching TV to be 50%, while the industry data puts the actual figure at just 19%.

So most people do not multi-screen while watching TV. This probably doesn't come as a huge surprise to those who live in the real world, but evidently some marketers live in a world of their own. And while we're all naturally inclined to make assumptions based on our own experience, the job of marketers is to understand the people in their market.

Beyond what it says about these marketers' lack of market orientation, this is also a neat example of a related problem in the marketing industry – namely, a preoccupation with all things digital.

You can barely look in the general direction of a marketing publication these days without being hit by a barrage of hype and hyperbole about digital.

Marketers continue to increase their investment in digital channels, which is a problem because it's influencing practice at the expense of marketing fundamentals.

As Melbourne Business School's Professor Mark Ritson has repeatedly pointed out, the notion of digitally led marketing is utterly inconsistent with the important marketing principle of media neutrality.

That is, no channels should be prioritised before the appropriate research has been done and a strategy formulated. To be digitally led is to put the tactical cart before the strategic horse.

What's more, the value of investing in some digital channels is questionable at best.

Online advertising is particularly dodgy. In the past couple of years, it has become clear that click-through rates on display ads are abominably low (0.06% on average), fraud is rampant and ad blocking is on the rise.

Meanwhile, a 2016 study by the American Marketing Association showed that more than 88% of marketing executives could not prove any quantitative impact of their social media marketing.

So if I am forced to take a side in the current debate between digital and traditional marketers – a silly distinction, but that's another topic – I'm firmly with the latter. I think marketers are much better off heeding the evidence-based wisdom of people such as Mark Ritson than believing the braggadocio of the digital gurus.

It's inevitable that digital channels will eventually become critical tools in brand building, given their growing presence in our daily lives. But we should remember that they are essentially channels like any other, and unlikely to be successful in isolation.

So will they change the fundamental principles of good marketing? In my opinion, no. After all, marketing is ultimately dependent on human behaviour and while the technologies will change, people won't.

As the legendary advertising man, Bill Bernbach, once said: "It took millions of years for man's instincts to develop. It will take millions more for them to even vary. A communicator must be concerned with unchanging man."

FACEBOOK WAS RECENTLY FOUND TO BE OVERSTATING SOME OF ITS METRICS BY AS MUCH AS 80%

This article was originally published in the Australian Financial Review's 'Boss' magazine.

THIS LITTLE PIGGY WENT TO MARKET. THIS LITTLE PIGGY STAYED HOME.

THIS LITTLE PIGGY ADVISED THE FIRST PIGGY ABOUT HOW TO LEVERAGE ITS FIRST-MOVER ADVANTAGE.

THIS LITTLE PIGGY WAS HIRED BY THE SECOND PIGGY TO DEVELOP A CHALLENGER BRAND STRATEGY.

AND THIS LITTLE PIGGY WENT "WE, WE, WE" BECAUSE IT WAS INSUFFICIENTLY CUSTOMER-CENTRIC.

DECISIONS
DECISIONS
DECISIONS

THE TOP TEN REASONS THAT MARKETERS GIVE FOR MAKING THEIR DECISIONS

1. That's what I would want if I was the customer.

2. My mate Dave thinks it's a great idea, and he's a smart guy.

3. That Shingy bloke said this is the future of marketing. At least I think that's what he said. I got a bit distracted by his hair.

4. One of the people in our focus group loved it. All the others hated it, but frankly I didn't like their attitude.

5. It's what Elon Zuckerberg-Branson does. I know because I saw a quote of his on LinkedIn.

6. I watched a TED talk about it. Actually I'm not sure what the talk was about exactly, but the speaker was really charismatic and inspiring. You should watch it.

7. Gary Vaynerchuk shouted it at me.

8. It was recommended at the Shiny New Things Echo Chamber conference.

9. Because Apple.

10. I use data. Wait, I mean feta. I use feta. Goes really well with spinach.

TNATEM

CJO
Chief Jargon Officer

Person who takes company-wide responsibility for the optimal implementation of linguistic over-complexificationism. Core competency is cross-sectoral alignment of value-adding communicative impenetrables.

RTC
Ridiculous Title Creator

One of the most important people in a marketing agency.

The RTC is responsible for transforming tradi-tional job titles like 'De-signer' (BORING!) into cutting-edge sobriquets such as 'Pixel ninja'.

ROG
Return On Gobbledygook

A financial measure particularly favoured by CJOs and BDBs.

Calculated by dividing net profit by the frequency of use of certain words in marketing communications (for example: 'leverage', 'value-adding', 'innovation').

The ROG acronym is best reserved for those who fully understand its role in leveraging value-adding innovation.

DTL
Down The Line

A contingency strategy activated in the event of a failed marketing campaign. As in: 'Our ATL and BTL activi-ties didn't work. We need to blame this on someone DTL.'

B2S
Business To Self

A type of marketing communication in which a business appears to be talking primarily to itself. Characterised by phrases such as 'We believe ...', 'That's why we ...', 'Our philosophy here at ...', and anything that refers to a 'journey'. B2S is sometimes abbreviated to just BS.

(THE NEW ACRONYMS THAT EVERY MARKETER MUST KNOW)

If there's one thing I'm sure we can all agree on, it's that there is a worrying dearth of impressive-sounding acronyms in our industry. So this is my attempt to add to the marketer's acronym arsenal (otherwise known as the 'arsenym').

CTI
Call To Inaction

An element of marketing communication that specifically and emphatically discourages a desired behaviour.

Common examples include QR codes, invitations to 'find out more about John's story online', and the phrase 'join the conversation'.

NFI
Newly Fabricated Institute

An attempt to confer gravitas on what would otherwise be an obvious re-hash of a marketing concept that's been around for decades.

The NFI phenomenon is characteristic of 'new-wave' marketers (which would make a good name for an institute, come to think of it).

BDB
Big Data Baffler

Someone who attempts to baffle you with big data (not ACTUAL big data – just the phrase 'big data').

Most BDBs have never studied statistics of any kind, and therefore think that a p-value refers to the monetary cost of relieving oneself in a European public convenience.

N2V
Noun To Verb

The practice of 'transitioning' a noun to a verb, on the basis that it implies more dynamism.

While not confined to any one industry, it has been embraced by marketers, who are especially partial to impacting, ideating and gamifying.

BLAH
BLAH
BLAH
BLAH

THE
CMO
QUOTE
GENERATOR

BLAH

Customers are at the

☐ heart

☐ core

☐ centre

of everything we do.

It's all about

☐ storytelling

☐ experiences

☐ engagement

Our new strategy is focused on

☐ influencers

☐ loyalists

☐ millennials

We want our brand to change the

☐ conversation

☐ culture

☐ world

We all know that

☐ advertising

☐ TV

☐ interruption

is dead.

Our approach is

☐ agile

☐ scalable

☐ disruptive

THE CHEAT'S GUIDE TO SENSIBLE MARKETING

There's no shortage of information about marketing out there – and there's even more misinformation. Faced with all this material (I dare not call it 'content'), sometimes you need to take a cognitive shortcut or two. Or in other words, you need to cheat. So here are some simple principles I follow, which you might find useful too.

1. Keep a salt shaker handy.

Because you'll need to take most of what you read with a grain of salt. Or 50.

2. Heed the words of the wise.

Read the blogs of Bob Hoffman, Dave Trott and George Tannenbaum. They are full of good sense and excellent writing. Not to mention some hilarious ranting.

3. Beware the prefix.

While there are notable exceptions, the addition of a prefix before the word 'marketing' is usually a warning that bullshit is in the offing. Social marketing, inbound marketing, relationship marketing and influencer marketing are at best new names for marketing approaches that have been around for decades.

4. Avoid overcomplication.

A set of brand guidelines does not need to be 200 pages long. A perceptual map does not need 10 dimensions. And as Mark Ritson says: if you can't define your brand in three words, you're doing a shit job.

5. Watch a video of the master.

David Ogilvy tells some home truths in the classic 'We sell or else'.

6. Don't be fooled by love.

Be very cautious about anything that refers to 'brand love' or even strong brand loyalty.

The notion that people fall in love with brands is mostly wishful thinking, and has been largely discredited by Byron Sharp in How Brands Grow.

7. Ignore reports from big consulting firms (unless you like parody).

8. If somebody proclaims something to be dead, refer back to number 1.

Advertising. Television. Direct mail.

Reports of their death have been greatly exaggerated (mostly by idiots).

9. Subscribe to Tom Fishburne's Marketoonist cartoons.

Not only are they sensible, but they will make you laugh.

And by God you do need to laugh at this industry sometimes.

FAMOUS
FAMOUS
FAMOUS
FAMOUS
FAMOUS
FAMOUS
FAMOUS
FAMOUS
FAMOUS

FAME
FAME
FAME

HOW TO BECOME
A FAMOUS MARKETER

1. First, choose a successful form of marketing that has been tried and tested over many decades.

2. Declare this form of marketing to be dead.

3. Justify this declaration on the basis that modern consumers are infinitely more intelligent than all who have come before them, and are therefore immune to traditional marketing. Do not feel obliged to support this assertion with any evidence.

4. Announce to the world that you have created a new form of marketing (or rather, a 'novel marketing paradigm'). This can be either:

A) The polar opposite of the one you have declared to be dead, or

B) Exactly the same as the one you have declared to be dead, but with a different name.

5. Give your new creation a catchy title that reflects the modern marketing zeitgeist. For the sake of argument, let's call it 'Sewer Marketing'.

6. Publish a book called Sewer Marketing.

7. Do a tour to promote yoursel... er, your book.

8. Bask in the effusive praise of gullible people.

VISIBILITY

2. Peak
of deluded hyperbole

3. Trough
of realisation that it's all a load of balls

1. Trigger
Some guru talking about
a 'disruptive innovation'

5. Plateau
of moving on to the next idiotic fad

THE MARKETING HYPE CYCLE

4. Slope
of pretending it's still great
so that more suckers buy it

TIME

THE FIVE STAGES
OF
MARKETING GRIEF

Denial	"I don't believe that evidence. It doesn't feel right."
Denial	"Although independent and methodologically impeccable, the research is biased."
Denial	"That data is hopelessly outdated – it's from last Tuesday."
Denial	"This can't be right because Tom, my 8 year-old nephew, doesn't do that."
Anger	"Just fuck off, you dinosaur."

10 THINGS THAT MARKETERS HAVE TAUGHT US ABOUT CENTENNIALS

1. First, the correct name for this generation is 'centennials'. This is an immutable fact, which exemplifies our certainty about these people.

2. Er, come to think of it, the correct name could be Gen Z. Or iGen. Look, it's not important, OK?

3. Centennials are different from millennials. For example, they are not subject to the breathless obsession of every marketer on the planet. Yet.

4. Despite having no money, centennials will soon be the most important target market in every category. This is because they are young and cool, and we want to be young and cool too.

5. Centennials are a completely homogeneous group. This may be because they are robots. We haven't confirmed this yet, as none of us has ever spoken to one.

6. Before marketing to centennials, you need to earn their respect. The easiest way to earn the respect of young people is to make sweeping generalisations about them.

7. Centennials hate advertising. This makes them unique, because people in other generations adore advertising.

8. Centennials will only deal with brands that have a clearly defined purpose. Worker exploitation, tax evasion, global domination – that kind of thing.

9. Centennials value authenticity above all else. Fortunately, you can learn how to feign authenticity at any marketing conference.

10. Centennials have very short attention spans and are easily distracted. Anyway, this is getting boring. Isn't there a new generation we can talk about?

FACTS
FACTS
FACTS

THE FACTS ABOUT GEN H
(GENERATION HUMAN)

1. Gen H comprises people born between 1900 and 2018.

2. Our research shows that they share the common trait of breathing.

3. People in this generation do certain things when they are younger, but then they get older and do other things. This groundbreaking insight is based on a multivariate analysis by a global consulting firm.

4. All members of Gen H are adamant that advertising has no effect on them.

5. Advertising has an effect on them.

6. It appears that people in Gen H like to have relationships with other people, rather than with brands. This disturbing possibility requires further validation.

7. Members of Gen H may demonstrate some degree of individual variation that can't be explained purely on the basis of when they were born. If this proves to be true, we'll ignore it.

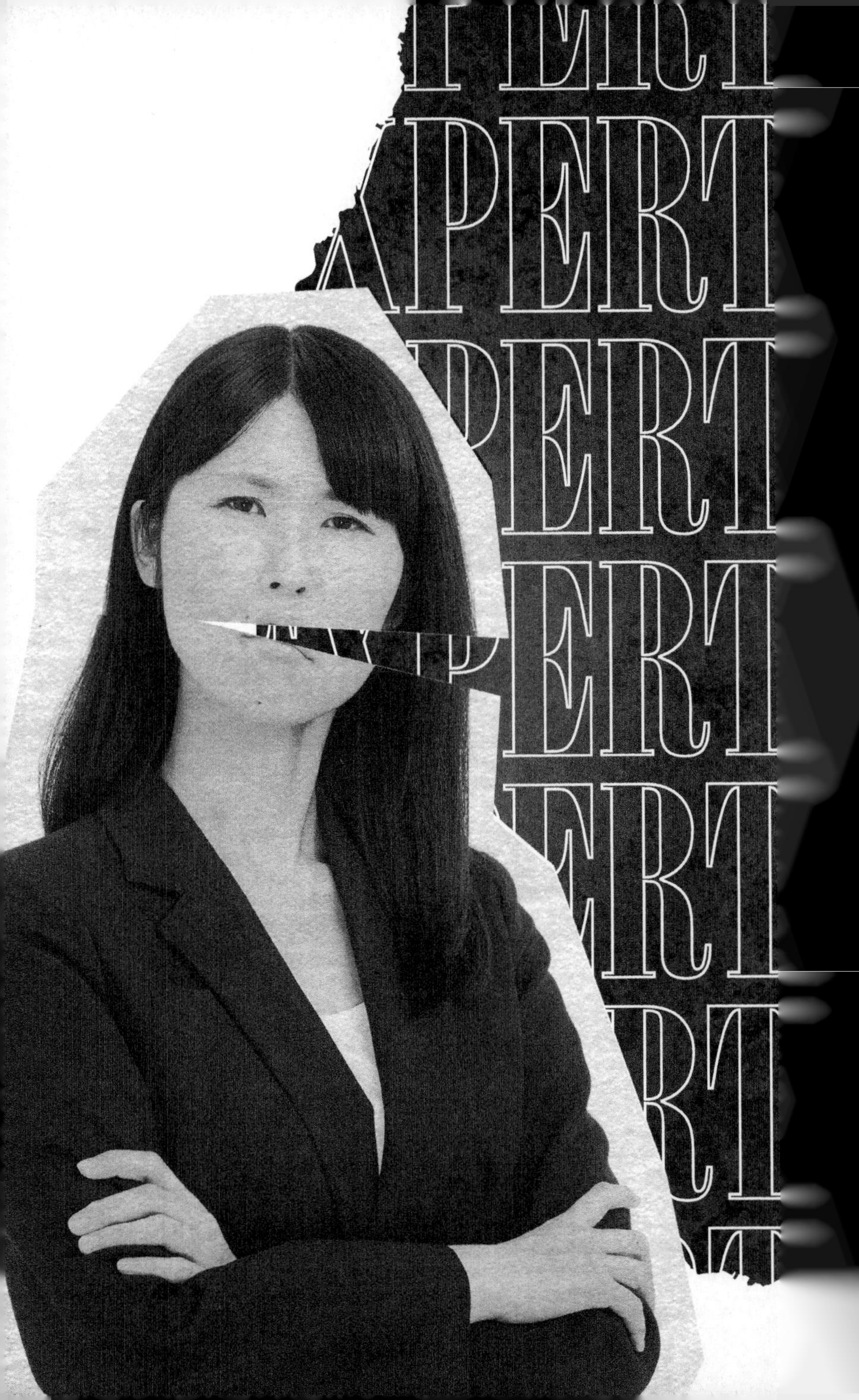

HOW TO BECOME A MARKETING EXPERT

1. First, let's be clear about one thing. You do NOT need any training to be a marketing expert.

2. If anyone questions this, cite the example of Richard Branson. Statistical considerations aside, this automatically wins you the argument.

3. Aggressively decry the expertise of people with so-called 'recognised credentials'. What the hell do those boffins know?

4. Insist that marketing has changed more in the last 10 minutes than it did in the previous 50 years.

5. It's probably a good idea to have some experience of marketing, but don't get hung up on the definition here. Marketing means whatever you want it to mean.

   You just do Snapchat strategies? Then you're a fully fledged marketing expert.

6. Forget esoterica like research, segmentation, positioning and all the rest of it. Modern marketing boils down to a) random digital stuff, and b) acronyms.

7. Once you have established yourself as an expert, make sure everyone knows it. The correct way to do this is to proclaim, at every available opportunity, that you are 'crushing it'.

THE PROBLEM	THE SOLUTION
LACK OF BRAND DISTINCTIVENESS	Change your logo typeface to Helvetica
LOW MARKET REACH	Invest your entire marketing budget in hyper-targeted Facebook ads
INSUFFICIENT CUSTOMER ACQUISITION	Start a loyalty program for your six best customers
LOW AWARENESS AMONG OLDER CONSUMERS	Create some cool TikTok memes
LIMITED ADVERTISING EFFECTIVENESS	Stop advertising altogether
LACK OF BRAND AUTHENTICITY	Hire a Kardashian to promote a worthy social cause that has no connection to your product
NO PROBLEM WHATSOEVER	Change your agency because of some moronic new policy introduced by Nigel from Procurement

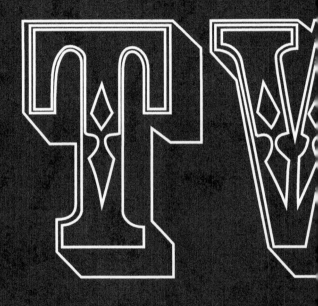

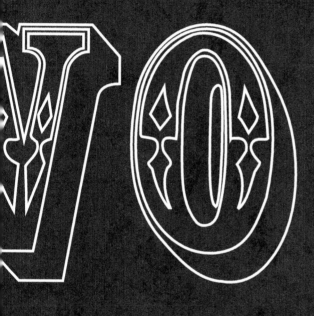

BRANDS

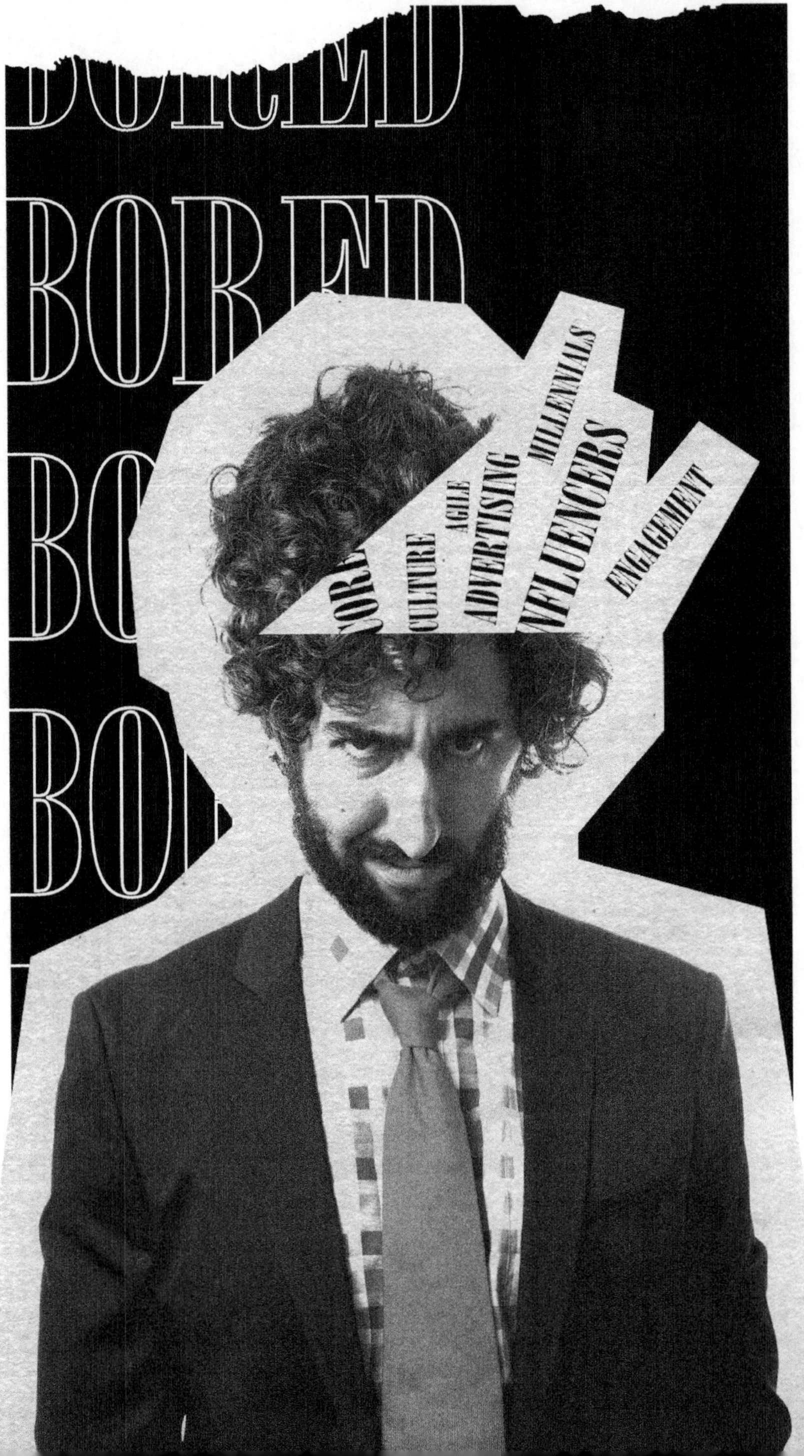
BORED
CULTURE
AGILE
ADVERTISING
MILLENNIALS
ENGAGEMENT

BORED OF YOUR BRAND? GOOD.

Sorry to break this to you, but people don't take much notice of you.

It's not just you, I should add. Generally speaking, people don't take much notice of anyone except themselves.

Knowing this can be quite liberating. In fact, it's used in the treatment of people who suffer from social anxiety.

A counselling service puts it this way:

"The reality is that most people are more interested in what is going on in their lives rather than thinking about you.

Other people probably take much less notice of you than you think."

That's the sobering truth about how people think. And I can assure you: they pay much less attention to brands than they do to other people.

So, if people are naturally inclined to take practically no notice of brands, what does that mean for your marketing?

It means you need to accept that your potential customers have better things to do than 'engage' with your brand.

You're always paying attention to your brand, but your customers aren't. They won't remember your brand after being exposed to it once or twice.

And that means you have to bore yourself.

You need to keep putting the same stuff out there – the same logo, the same colours, the same tagline – over and over again.

These are the distinctive brand assets (to use Byron Sharp's term) that cue your brand to a largely uninterested audience. And they can only

be built by consistent use over time.

To be clear, this is not to say that your communications themselves should all be the same. That will only exacerbate the risk of their being glossed over.

I think this quote from How Brands Grow 2 explains the situation perfectly: "Advertise messages for the short term but build a brand identity for the long term. Mixing the two makes it more difficult to achieve either."

So resist the temptation to create a 'fresh identity' every few years. Forget rebranding (unless there's a very good reason for it) and reinvention and all the rest of it.

Your primary goal should be to get your brand noticed and keep it noticed.

Much better to be bored than ignored.

ONCE UPON A TIME

Once upon a time, there was a little brand.

This little brand felt glum. It wanted to be a big brand.

Everyone told the little brand that to become a big brand, it would need to build relationships with millennials in an authentic way.

They assured the little brand that anything else would be a complete waste of time, because advertising is dead.

So the little brand tried to have conversations with young people, but the young people said things like "why the hell would I want to talk to you?" and "fuck off, little brand". This made the little brand sad.

But the little brand persisted. It knew in its heart that people wanted brands to do good things for the world, like sympathise with the latest political trend on Twitter.

And the little brand also knew that it should never do bad things like try to sell its products.

The little brand died. **The end.**

5	88	7	110
B	**Ra**	**N**	**Ds**
Boron	Radium	Nitrogen	Darmstadtium
10.81	[226]	14.007	[281]

A BREAKTHROUGH IN THE SCIENCE OF BRANDING

Introducing a totally new branding paradigm from Unqualified Leads – your full-spectrum, omni-channel, 360-rotational, navel-visicentric brand consultancy.

Forget everything you thought you knew about marketing. All that stuff in your stuffy head is just stuff and nonsense. Luckily for you, it won't be there for long because we're about to blow your mind.

We've developed a branding game-changer – one that changes the game from what that last game-changer changed the game to. So put on your game face.

It's called Brand Nucleotide®. And it will revolutionise the way you do business.

What is Brand Nucleotide?

Nucleotides are the building blocks of DNA (we looked that up on Wikipedia), so Brand Nucleotide is like the purified essence of brand DNA. How does it differ from brand DNA? It adds greater value, because it's more *fundamental* – and also because we've trademarked it.

But let's not get into too much 'granularity' here. The point is that Brand Nucleotide sounds way more scientific than brand DNA, which makes it better. It's kind of like the difference between Big Data and un-big, un-capitalised, un-sexy data. And needless to say, Brand Nucleotide is fully informed by Big Data. It's all about Big Data, in fact. Big Data Big Data Big Data. (Sorry, just optimising our keywords.)

So do we have any scientific qualifications, you ask? Erm, well, not as such. In fact, we never got past year 8 science. That's what gives us an edge, you see, because it allows us to think outside the box of so-called 'rational thought'.

And no, we're not marketers exactly – not in the trained sense. But we've got, you know, real-world experience. With brands and all that. We've done heaps of work on Apple. Of course we have. What self-respecting agency bod would use a PC?

But what's that? You want to know whether Brand Nucleotide gets results? Hmm, that's a bit too much like conventional science for us. Our CodScience™ theoretical model doesn't extend to outcomes. Anyway, if you want results, just look them up in Big Data or something.

How does Brand Nucleotide work?

Ah, well, to find that out, you'll have to buy the Brand Nucleotide Premium Package – for only a little more than what scientists spent on sequencing the human genome.

Buy now, before someone clones our idea.

BRAND LOVE

BRAND BOLLOCKS

AGENDA

BRAND PLANNING WORKSHOP*

9.00	Unnecessary introductions
9.15	Presentation of biased market research results
10.00	AWKWARD MORNING TEA
10.30	Some bollocks about emotional laddering
11.00	Breakout groups: Meaningless diagrams on butcher's paper that nobody will ever look at again
12.00	LUNCH (OPPORTUNITY TO IGNORE EACH OTHER WHILE STARING AT SCREENS)
1.00	Hypothetical game based on an inappropriate military metaphor
2.00	Three hours discussing the tagline 'Progress is our passion' (more time available if needed)
5.00	Agreement on next steps that will never happen because everybody will be too busy planning next year's workshop

*Subject to change depending on the number of irrelevant digressions by the guy from head office who loves the sound of his own voice

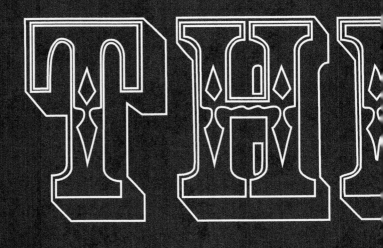

REE

MANY YEARS AGO –
TOO MANY FOR MY
LIKING – THERE WAS A TV
COMMERCIAL FOR A BRAND
OF GARDEN SPRINKLER.

NO, WAIT.
IT GETS BETTER, I PROMISE.

THE
SILENT
AD
THAT
SPOKE
VOLUMIES

This ad was remarkable.

It wasn't famous, mind you. You won't have read about it in advertising textbooks, and I doubt that it would have won any awards.

In fact, it was for a fairly obscure Australian brand that you've probably never heard of. Unless you lived in Perth in the 1980s. (If so: my condolences.)

Anyway, the remarkable thing about this ad was that nothing really happened. And it was silent.

The ad was little more than a black screen overlaid by a super that read (something to the effect of): "This is the sound of one of our sprinklers". It ended with a shot of a lush lawn.

Aside from the fact that it neatly demonstrated a benefit of the product, the really striking aspect of this ad was that it stood in stark contrast to everything around it. All of the other ads at that time, and indeed most

of the TV programs, were loud and tacky. It was the '80s, after all.

In that context, this unassuming little ad was almost impossible to ignore.

And it made a huge impression on me at the time. Funnily enough, I can still remember thinking "I would like to go into advertising so that I can make an ad like that". Which is saying a lot, because gardening products interest me approximately as much as whitepapers on programmatic marketing.

So would that ad work today? In this era when all available space must be filled?

I think it would. Given the bluster and blather of advertising in the 21st century, such a simple idea would probably be more effective than ever.

Because for all the 'noise' that characterises modern marketing – the convoluted strategies, data dashboards, media plans, contextualised

targeting, concept testing and what have you – the single most important rule of advertising is that it must be noticed.

This rule does not change with the times. It will always be true that if an ad doesn't get noticed, it is pointless. Totally, utterly pointless.

Consider the last ad that you put out there. And be honest with yourself. If you saw that ad, would it stop you in your tracks?

If your answer is something like "Probably not, but the message is on-brand and the images are correctly placed in accordance with our style guidelines": you've got a problem.

Nobody looking at your ad has your brief on hand. Nobody is checking it off against your strategy or wondering about your message hierarchy or measuring the height of your logo.

Indeed, the difference between how you see your ad and how your audience sees it might be summarised thus…

HMM, I'M NOT SURE ABOUT THAT HEADLINE–IMAGE COMBO. MIGHT BE TOO OBVIOUS. AND THE HEADLINE GETS LOST. IT NEEDS TO BE ABOUT 4 POINT SIZES BIGGER. I WOULDN'T HAVE USED CALIBRI, PERSONALLY. AND THAT KERNING NEEDS WORK. COULD DO WITH A TOUCH MORE WHITE SPACE. SURELY THE SUPPORTING COPY IS REDUNDANT? I DON'T THINK THE USE OF BORROWED INTEREST REALLY WORKS. AND THAT LOGO ISN'T ANCHORED PROPERLY. MIND YOU, THE PAYOFF LINE ISN'T BAD. REMINDS ME A BIT OF THAT CAMPAIGN FROM LAST YEAR. I WONDER WHO DID IT. I THINK TOM'S AGENCY DOES THEIR STUFF, COME TO THINK OF IT...

WHAT EVERYONE ELSE THINKS
WHEN THEY SEE AN AD:

ISN'T THE TV GUIDE
SUPPOSED TO BE HERE?

SO THE FIRST QUESTION TO ASK ABOUT ANY ADVERTISING IS

WILL IT BE NOTICED?

Then, sure, ask the other important questions. Is this the right message? Is the ad believable? Does it demonstrate the benefits? Is there a strong incentive? And so on.

But if the answer to that first question is "no", all of those other questions are irrelevant.

If the answer is "yes", on the other hand, then your message might get through. It might be remembered. It might be written about some 30 years later.

Hell, it might even inspire a career.

THE ADVERTISING DEVELOPMENT PROCESS

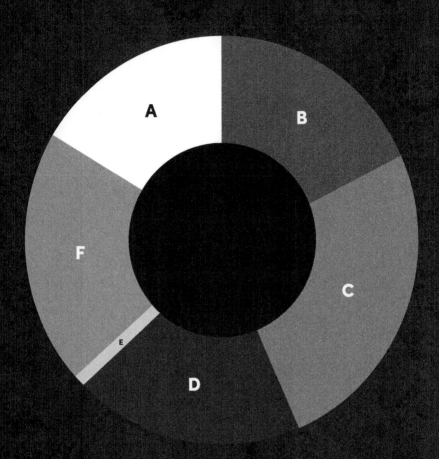

A Award submission

B Reading the 50-page brief

C Overthinking

D Design by committee

E Creating the ad

F Post-rationalisation

MANIFESTO
MANIFESTO
MANIFESTO

A MINI-MANIFESTO FOR OUR INDUSTRY

We ought to be thinking in terms of ideas, not gadgets.

We should prioritise efficacy, not efficiency.

We must be concerned with what is timeless, not what is trending.

We ought to question the orthodoxy, not acquiesce to it.

We should be motivated by results, not awards.

We must use vital language, not deadened cliches.

We ought to nurture talent, not "manage talent".

We should look to the lessons of the past, not the vagaries of the future.

We ought to be informed by data, not enthralled by it.

And we must always, always be wary of prescriptive advice.

THE REAL ADVERTISING AWARDS

The Groomed Beard Award
For the most solipsistic use of ironic humour in an advertising campaign

The Great Brain Robbery Award
For the most brazen theft of someone else's idea

The Golden Bollocks Award
For the most ridiculous jargon used to win an account

The Lipstick on a Pig Award
For the best case study video of an otherwise awful campaign

The Dad You're Embarrassing Me Award
For the most cringeworthy use of emojis in an advertising campaign

The Busy Hand Award
For the most self-congratulatory article in an industry publication

The WTF Award
For the most incomprehensible new industry acronym

The Simulated Lobotomy Award
For the most mentions of 'millennials' in an industry blog

The Delusions of Brandeur Award
For the advertising agency that most vehemently denies being an advertising agency

The Grand Prick Award
For the most obnoxious delegate at an advertising festival

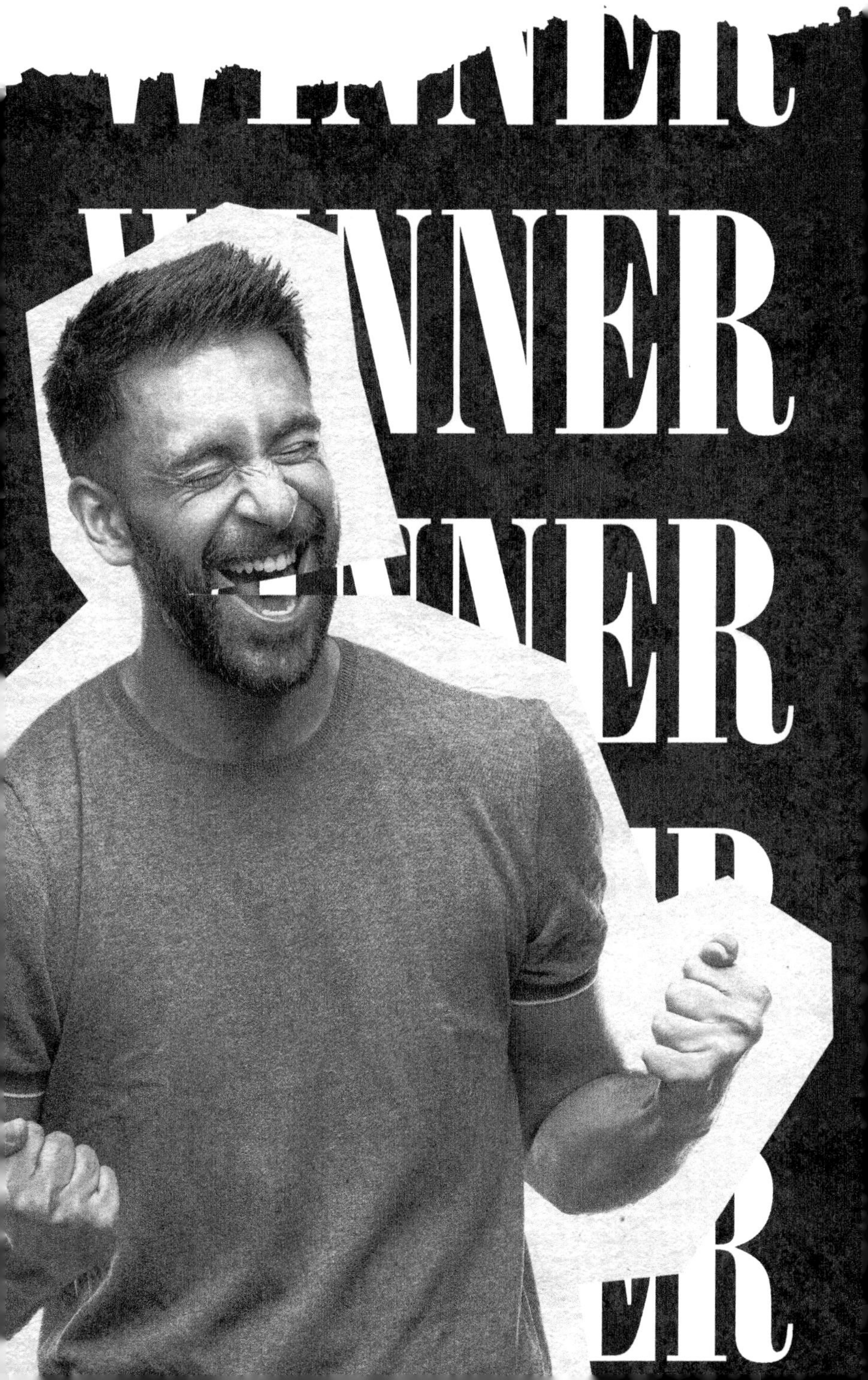
NNER
NNER
ER

TO ACHIEVE WHAT OUTCOME?
WHAT WILL WE BE MEASURED ON?
I THINK YOU'RE HAVING A STROKE

MEDMEN

BEFORE I
BECAME A WRITER,
I WAS A DOCTOR.
THAT STORY WOULD
BORE YOU, SO I WON'T
DWELL ON IT.

But recently, while reflecting on my change of tack, I wondered: what if medicine was like the advertising industry?

I'll call this hypothetical industry "medland". Let me tell you a bit about medland.

Modern medland was born in the 1950s, thanks to a group of revolutionary practitioners on Medicine Avenue.

Since then, however, times and tastes have changed. Medland is a very different place these days.

In today's medland, doctors never talk to patients. There's no need, you see. They just treat all patients the same way, by assuming everyone is a 20 year-old athlete in rude health. They justify this by saying that everyone WANTS to be a 20 year-old athlete in rude health.

So if you're an 80 year-old nursing home resident, your doctors might not fix your broken hip, but they'll give you some rock-solid advice about

how to optimise your muscle recovery after your next triathlon.

One reason for this is that the doctors themselves are all young people in rude health. Most doctors in medland are under the age of 30, and almost all are forced out of medicine by 40. This makes sense, according to hospital spokespeople, because "only young doctors are savvy enough to understand the needs of tomorrow's patients, today".

And of course hospitals need to keep up with the times, too. For example, no self-respecting hospitals in medland still refer to themselves as hospitals. They are now "betterness hubs" or "full-spectrum wellbeing incubators".

The services offered by hospitals have also been re-named. What used to be called ophthalmology is now known as "VXA" (or "visual experience augmentation"), and orthopaedic surgery is a "multi-bonal alignment solution".

Meanwhile, hospitals now refer to their collection of services as "end-to-end" (although this initially caused some confusion because patients thought it meant gastroenterology).

That said, many hospitals in medland no longer provide a full range of medical services, preferring to focus exclusively on the treatment of fingers – i.e. all things digital.

So-called traditional doctors, trained in complete human anatomy, have been replaced by finger specialists. There is even a "digital prophet", who makes wild predictions about the future of finger health despite having no medical credentials.

One notable aspect of medland is that doctors must win a lot of awards before they are taken seriously.

Fortunately, there are many chances to win awards, and hardly any awards are judged according to patient outcomes.

A horribly botched brain operation, for example, could still win an award if it was beautifully filmed with some stirring music in the background.

Not uncommonly, a major award will be given to a procedure that wasn't done in a real hospital, or did not involve a patient.

This happened only last year when a Grand Prix was awarded to a surgeon who later confessed that he was actually playing the children's game "Operation".

The judges defended their decision on the basis that "it was a creative use of gamification that really engaged young people".

Doctors in medland also attend a lot of conferences. This is not so they can learn from their expert colleagues, mind you – that would be narrow-minded and limiting.

The speakers at medland conferences are people with no experience of medicine at all, such as celebrities.

Sometimes these celebrities are even appointed as Medical Directors of major hospitals.

So, as you can tell, medland is a strange place indeed.

Truly mad.

How modern advertising works (according to people in advertising)

1. Trendy Millennial sees a viral campaign for Ultracool Brand. She is engaged by its freshness, innovation and alignment with her inner-urban lifestyle.

2. In response to the campaign, Trendy Millennial takes a selfie and posts it on social media with a #pointlesshashtag.

3. Trendy Millennial 'joins the conversation' related to #pointlesshashtag.

4. This co-creation experience inspires Trendy Millennial to visit Ultracool Brand's website to find out more about their Story. She is captivated.

5. Exploring the Ultracool Brand website further, Trendy Millennial is highly impressed by their Total Commitment to Social Responsibility.

She is therefore prepared to overlook the fact that Ultracool Brand's products are made from the blood of endangered species by chain-smoking 5-year-olds in medieval dungeons.

6. Trendy Millennial falls head-over-heels in love with Ultracool Brand.

7. Trendy Millennial becomes an evangelical advocate for Ultracool Brand. She is now an Influencer.

How modern advertising actually works

1. Person sees an ad for Brand on TV.

2. When Person is next in a buying situation, Person is somewhat more likely to buy Brand.

A SHOCKING ROLE MODEL FOR YOUR ADVERTISING

Some time ago, my uncle played me a recording of Derek and Clive, Peter Cook and Dudley Moore's famously crude radio show.

Now, when I say it was crude, I mean it was *CRUDE*. Look it up if you don't believe me.

And when I say it was some time ago, I mean I was four years old.

Suffice it to say, then, that I was probably a touch too young for the material. My grandmother certainly seemed to think so when she walked in on the scene.

But according to my uncle – who still can't recount this story without (sheepishly) laughing – that's what made it so hilarious. Having absolutely no idea what any of it meant, I recited my own version of the recording. Replete with every four-letter word you can imagine, and a few besides.

In other words, the incongruity of the situation made it funny. Just as it did in a great ad for Smart cars a couple of years ago, which also featured swearing kids.

There's no doubt that incongruity can be a powerful device in advertising.

Think of the famous VW 'Lemon' ad or, to take a more recent example, the Snickers 'You're not you when you're hungry' campaign.

And yet so much modern advertising seems to actively eschew incongruity.

Stock images. Young people. Platitudes. All in banal, boring harmony.

Such ads are not only internally congruous, but externally congruous as well. That is, they look the same as every other ad. It's almost as if there has been a deliberate attempt to prevent them from standing out.

To illustrate this problem, here's a briefing template I put together a while ago.

What *tone* do you want to strike?

☐ Boring

☐ Pretentious

☐ Condescending

What *tagline* do you want to use?

☐ Making a difference

☐ Leading innovation

☐ Tomorrow's {your category} today

What *image* do you want to include?

☐ Stock photo of attractive man in suit

☐ Stock photo of attractive woman staring into the middle distance

☐ People looking ecstatic for no apparent reason

What *call-to-action* do you want to use?

☐ Find out more

☐ Discover our story

☐ Join the conversation

At the risk of stating the obvious, this bland uniformity is no way to get your advertising noticed. It's certainly no way to elicit an emotional reaction. And as for getting a laugh: when was the last time you laughed at something you completely expected?

A bit of incongruity can greatly improve your advertising. I swear by it.

HONEST LISTS FOR THE ADVERTISING INDUSTRY

The 3 People In Advertising Who Are Over The Age of 50

The 4.2 Million People In Advertising Who Have Nothing To Do With The Creation Of Advertising

The 7 People In Advertising Who Have Ever Seen An Ad Made Before 1990

The 12 People In Advertising Who Understand The Basic Principles Of Marketing

The 93,000 People In Advertising Who Refer To Themselves As Freelance Creative Directors

The 8 Men In Advertising Who Don't Have Facial Hair

The 4 Women In Advertising Who Have Never Been Subjected To Sexual Discrimination

The 2.7 Million People In Advertising Who Have Never Spoken To Anyone Outside Advertising

The 8 People In Advertising Who Create Ads For Non-Millennials

The 2 People In Advertising Who Have Conservative Political Views

RIP
ADVERTISING

IN LOVING MEMORY OF ADVERTISING

Died in 2018, 2017, 2016 and 2015 depending on which expert you listen to.

Advertising enjoyed great success during its long life, but finally succumbed to the ravages of corporate bullshit and technological obsession. Its happy marriage to Media ended acrimoniously when Media got into bed with Precision Targeting.

Advertising is survived by its bastard offspring, Content Marketing and Influencer Marketing. Its final message to them was "good luck achieving anything without me, you obnoxious little prats".

There will be no funeral service, and all you gurus who have been waiting for this day are asked to refrain from dancing on the grave.

THE AD DICTIONARY

Ad gustum
Advertising to one's own taste. This usually means 'to the taste of obnoxious 22-year-old white males'.

Ad hoc
Advertising created to overcome a specific problem. Nowadays, that problem is always how to get through to millennials, using emojis.

Ad hominem
An ad campaign that targets the stereotypical traits of a customer, rather than what they might actually think. Favoured by those who treat buyer personas as gospel (or 'idiots', to use an ad hominem description of them).

Ad ignorantium
Advertising that's ignorant of the principles of good marketing. So pretty much all of it.

Ad infinitum
An ad campaign that seemingly runs forever. For the general public, this means decades. For marketers, it means the 3 weeks before they lose patience and decide that a new campaign (and agency) is needed.

Ad lib
Advertising that appears to have been run without anybody giving it a single prior thought. Generally applies to ads for perfume.

Ad nauseam
An ad campaign that is either a) so bad that it makes you want to vomit, or b) endlessly repetitive. In keeping with Sod's Law, it's almost always both.

Ad tech
Latin term for 'total clusterfuck that makes people hate advertising'.

STAYING
HUMAN
WITHIN
THE
MACHINE

When I was a medical student, I read a book called The House of God. It was, to say the least, an eye-opener.

If you don't know The House of God, it is a satirical account of an intern as he navigates the strange world of hospital medicine. By turns cynical, hilarious, tender and depressing, it's practically a bible for junior doctors.

The reason it is so popular, I suspect, is that it's funny but also frighteningly true.

To give you an example, one of the "laws" of the House of God is: "At a cardiac arrest, the first procedure is to take your own pulse".

When you're an intern, The House of God feels like a pretty accurate account of your job – particularly the way that its constant demands can alienate you from the very people you're meant to be helping. Despite the caring nature of the role, there can be an odd detachment that one experiences as a young doctor.

Put it this way. It's hard – if not professionally impossible – to feel deeply for every patient you see when you have a list of 60 names to review by the end of your 15-hour overnight shift. When your pager is buzzing. When you can't get that bloody IV line in. And when you're worrying about whether you wrote the wrong dose of heart medication for the patient you just saw.

In other words, it can be a dehumanising experience.

Nevertheless, there are times when the raw humanity of the job smashes its way into your consciousness. I once looked after a patient with terminal cancer – a truly lovely lady – who died in front of me after weeks of suffering. Some 17 years later, the memory of her final hours still haunts me.

Ultimately, this contrast between personal connection and systemic disconnection is what the House of God is really about.

Samuel Shem, the author, reflected on his influential book 34 years after its publication:

"Some have said that The House of God is cynical. And yet in rereading, it has a constant message that I was dimly conscious of in writing: being with the patient."

For me, this reinforced the need to stay human at work. It's profoundly important for people in healthcare, of course, but it applies to every field to some extent. The recent suicides of overworked young people in advertising agencies have served as a sad reminder that even our own industry can grind people down.

Notwithstanding our obsession with technology and chatbots and AI and all the other substitutes we have for humanity, our work is still mostly done by people. For now, at least, we need to take care of them.

10 THINGS FOR WHICH HISTORY WILL JUDGE US HARSHLY / QR CODES / INSTAGRAM INFLUENCERS / THE PHRASE 'JOIN THE CONVERSATION' / THE PHRASE 'ADVERTISING IS DEAD' / CHIEF MARKETING OFFICERS WHO TALK INCESSANTLY ABOUT BRAND PURPOSE / BRAND PURPOSE / LINKEDIN ENDORSEMENTS / LINKEDIN NOTIFICATIONS / PRETTY MUCH EVERYTHING ABOUT LINKEDIN, COME TO THINK OF IT / LISTS ENTITLED '10 THINGS...'

IMPORTANT ANNOUNCEMENT FROM THE CEO OF [AGENCY NAME]

As part of **[AGENCY NAME]**'s commitment to reimagining the agency model for a future-forward society, we are delighted to announce the launch of our new division: **[AGENCY NAME]** Blockchain.

[AGENCY NAME] Blockchain offers full-service, end-to-end, blockchain-based solutions via a real-time iterative global platform. It represents an evolutionary pivot to the demands of innovative modern businesses.

To accommodate **[AGENCY NAME]** Blockchain, we are realigning our internal resources to ensure we have the world's best blockchain talent. The first step in this process will be the de-employmenting of our entire creative department. To help facilitate this structural orientationing, I will be taking a substantially bigger salary role going forward.

In summary, blockchain.

Sincerely

[NAME]
Chief Executive Officer
[AGENCY NAME]

ROADSIDE ADVERTISING:

Too much copy to read safely

Flimsy premise

Irrelevant inclusion of an animal

Tautological claim

THE WARNING SIGNS.

Minimal inclination to act

Inappropriate sexual innuendo

Excessive punctuation

Just utter bull

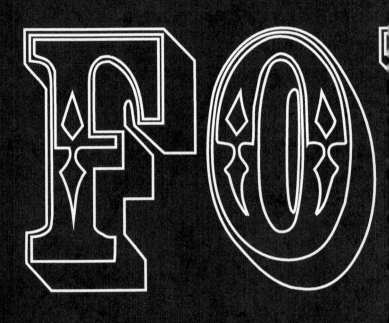

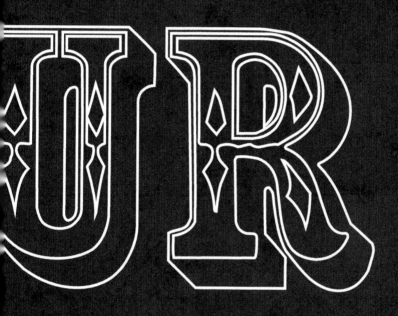

CREATIVITY

HOW TO BE
CREATIVE

Define the problem that you need to solve.

↓

Stare out of the window.

↓

Take a break.

↓

Stare at a computer screen.

↓

Go outside for a change of scene.

↓

Stare at a blank notebook.

↓

Go to bed.

↓

Stare at the ceiling.

↓

Just as you're drifting off, have the most extraordinarily brilliant idea in the history of humanity.

↓

Wake up with no recollection of the idea.

FOR THE CREATIVE THINKER, THE DEVIL*

*IS IN THE DETAIL

WHEN IT COMES TO ART, I FALL INTO THE "DON'T KNOW MUCH BUT I KNOW WHAT I LIKE" CATEGORY. IN OTHER WORDS, I'M EMBARRASSINGLY IGNORANT ABOUT IT.

So I was recently fascinated to hear the technical rationale behind Auguste Rodin's famous sculpture 'The Thinker'. Anyone with so much as a passing knowledge of fine art would probably consider this information elementary, but it was news to me.

I've always liked The Thinker, perhaps because it's such an easily 'accessible' work. Even to the casual observer, it is obvious that this sculpture represents someone in a deeply contemplative state. But what is not so obvious – or wasn't to me, at least – is the detail that enables this to be conveyed with such apparent effortlessness.

I'm told that the key to The Thinker's immediately understandable pose is two-fold.

First, the subject is naked. This is crucial because it means that his muscles are visible.

Second, his right elbow rests on his left knee. This may seem a trivial detail, and many observers probably don't even notice it. But its importance can be appreciated if you try this yourself – and realise that it is neither a comfortable nor natural position. It takes effort.

Because of this, The Thinker's muscles are visibly taut, which gives observers the unmistakeable impression of a man deep in thought.

What I find intriguing about this is that none of it was in any way serendipitous. These details were not happy accidents: Rodin knew exactly what he was doing.

You don't need to be an aficionado to realise that The Thinker is the work of a master. But it's the elements that contribute to this mastery that really get to the nub of Rodin's creative genius.

Knowing how people will emotionally respond to something.

Understanding the subtle, almost imperceptible details that will elicit this response.

And then weaving it all together with the painstaking dedication of a craftsman.

Now *that* is a truly creative thinker.

CREATIVE AWARDS RULES FOR ENTRY

1. Generally speaking, your entry should not have been created for a paying client. If it was, then the client must have no knowledge of the work.

2. In the unlikely event that your entry appeared in the public domain, it must have run only in a self-published fanzine or as a one-off supplement in Tasmanian Lumberjack Monthly.

3. Your entry must not be submitted as it actually appeared. Prior to submission, it should be stripped of all unsightly distractions, such as copy.

4. Entries promoting a product or service, rather than a fashionable social cause, will not be considered.

5. Print campaigns that do not include a visual pun will be disqualified.

6. Your entry must be completely incomprehensible to the average person. The judges will only award work that takes a team of military code-breakers several hours to decipher.

7. The importance of your case study cannot be overstated. Even the most abysmal work stands a chance if your case study is lavishly produced and has some impressive-sounding numbers in it.

8. Every entry must credit a minimum of 45 people, including at least three Global Chiefs. Crediting the copywriter or art director is optional.

MARKETERS
MUST LOOSEN
THEIR GRIP
ON THE
CREATIVE
PROCESS

IN CASE YOU HADN'T NOTICED, IT'S CREATIVE AWARDS SEASON. CANNES LIONS HAS JUST COME AND GONE FOR ANOTHER YEAR, WITH ALL THE HYPE AND HUBRIS THAT GOES ALONG WITH IT.

But what does it all mean for marketers? Should you give a flying fornication about the creativity of your agency, let alone whether they win any awards for it?

The answer, as with almost everything in marketing, is that it depends.

Before we get into the reasons for that, I should declare my bias here. I work for a creative agency, so naturally I have a vested interest in the value of creative work. But I've also been a fairly vocal critic of creativity for its own sake (or 'creative wank' to use the scientific term), so I would like to think I'm relatively balanced on this issue. Plus, I haven't won many awards – on principle, of course.

Anyway, this is about you. How much should you concern yourself with the creative work that supports your marketing?

In answering that question, it's worth keeping in mind that creativity is a mercurial concept. Because it's not easy to measure, it tends to be a source of buttock-clenching anxiety for what Ogilvy's Rory Sutherland refers to as "the arithmocracy". And so, inevitably, the people who control the purse strings have put an increasing focus on creative outputs that can be measured, which has led us to the siren calls of precision targeting and digital metrics and assorted ad tech flimflammery.

Proving the value of creativity

While it's difficult to assess overall creativity numerically, there is some pretty convincing evidence to demonstrate its value.

Exhibit A, which has featured on several industry blogs of late, is from a 2014 study by Admap. This research, based on an analysis of more than 1,500 case studies, ranked the top 10 factors that drive advertising profitability.

Creative execution was the second largest contributor to advertising profitability after market size. Nothing to be scoffed at, then. As strategist Tom Roach says: "Creative execution is not 'colouring in'. It matters more than nearly everything else."

This finding was echoed in a 2017 Nielsen analysis of advertising effectiveness, based on nearly 500 campaigns across all media platforms.

In this analysis, creative quality was easily the most important factor for generating sales, contributing more than double the next highest factor (reach).

Meanwhile, targeting –supposedly the cure for all ills in modern marketing – was one of the least important factors.

So it's science, innit. The quality of creative work is clearly important if you're interested in increasing profits and sales. Which you are, presumably.

But what of creative awards? Do they tell you anything besides which French rosé is de rigueur this year?

Even among agency folk, creative awards are polarising. The big awards shows tend to be characterised by 'ads for ad people' – work focused primarily on winning awards rather than being effective in the real world.

However, that might be a false dichotomy. According to Les Binet and Peter Field's work for the IPA, creatively awarded campaigns are more efficient at driving market share growth than non-awarded campaigns (see bottom left).

It's worth noting that this research has generated some debate in recent times. In an intriguing article for BBH Labs, Harry Guild questioned the role of survivorship bias in Binet and Field's findings. He argued that the analysed campaigns may not be representative of campaigns in general, since "nobody's entering dross into the IPA".

In response to that article, Binet acknowledged the limitations of the research, but pointed out that other research institutes such as Ehrenberg-Bass and Nielsen have reached similar conclusions.

At the very least, the IPA findings suggest that highly awarded work is more effective than less awarded work. And as Binet puts it: "By comparing the good with the better with the best, you just might learn a thing or two about how to improve your game."

To state what may seem obvious, marketers can benefit from good creative work – and can benefit even more from great work.

Which brings us to the thorny issue of how to know whether creative work is great, good, bad or 'Kendall Jenner-Pepsi'. And, ideally, to know this before the work is exposed to an unforgiving world.

No problem, right? All you need to do is some creative pre-testing.

Not so fast.

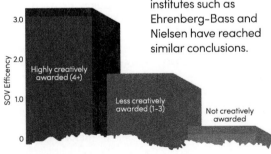

SOV Efficency

3.0

2.0

1.0

0

Highly creatively awarded (4+)

Less creatively awarded (1-3)

Not creatively awarded

Source (Left): Les Binet and Peter Field, Selling Creativity Short, IPA

Unfortunately, pre-testing can't predict how people will actually respond to creative work. As David Ogilvy once quipped: "The problem with market research is that people don't think how they feel, they don't say what they think and they don't do what they say."

In fact, Peter Field has demonstrated a negative correlation between the use of quantitative pre-testing and the success of IPA award entries. This implies that if you use quantitative methods to pre-test your creative work, you might be doing the opposite of what you intend, thereby reducing its likelihood of success.

The evidence for qualitative pre-testing is more anecdotal, but there are many examples of great campaigns that almost didn't happen because of such testing. As Lucian Trestler recently noted: "some of the most effective ideas of all time were slaughtered in qual".

So if you can't rely on pre-testing, what can you do?

This answer will probably disappoint you, but my recommendation is that you loosen your grip on the creative process. Creative work is like a rebellious teenager – the more you try to control it, the less it will do what you want.

With that in mind, the first step is to give your agency some space. Brief them well, then let them do their thing.

Second, remember that it doesn't really matter whether you 'like' the creative work or not. What matters is how your customers respond to it.

And third, don't analyse the work to death. It will inevitably lead to compromise, and the end result will be anodyne (or worse).

If you provide the right conditions for good creative work, the work will reward you.

Trust me – I'm a doctor.

This article was originally published in Marketing Week.

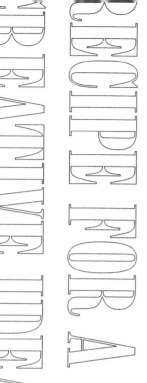

RECIPE FOR A CREATIVE IDEA

Step 1: Before starting on your creative idea, be sure to pre-heat your brain. Do not attempt this recipe until you have allowed at least two caffeine-based beverages to take effect.

Step 2: Mix together an eclectic assortment of books, artistic influences and life experiences, and combine the resulting mixture with your imagination. You should start to see some links forming.

Step 3: Allow this mixture to marinate in your subconscious overnight.

Step 4: If you happen to wake during the night and your creative idea is ready, for God's sake don't just leave it. If you do, you'll wake in the morning to find that it has completely disintegrated.

Step 5: After the overnight marination process, your creative idea may be fully formed. However, it can take a little longer for this to occur - anywhere between 5 minutes and several years.

Step 6: If there is no sign of an idea at this stage, go for a walk. You might be surprised at the progress when you return.

Step 7: If your creative idea still hasn't developed, it's time to give it a little help. We suggest four shots of vodka, but any reasonably potent intoxicant will suffice.

Step 8: Repeat Step 7 until the idea rises to the surface. Note, however, that it may become increasingly difficult to tell whether the idea is any good.

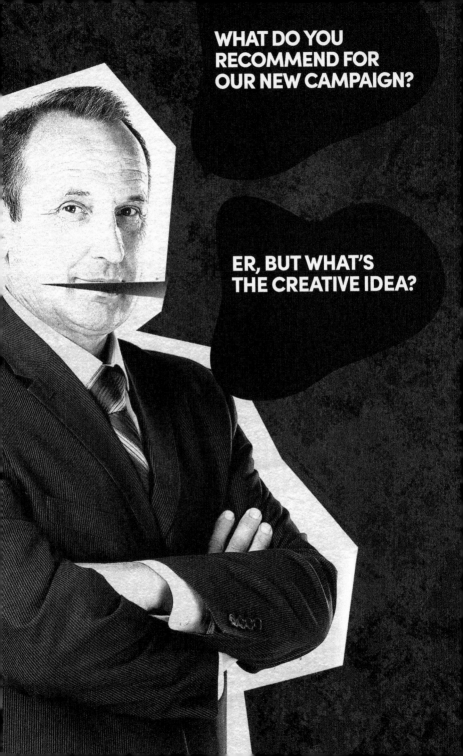

THE CURIOUS CASE OF A CREATIVE GENIUS

I went to school with a guy who could well be the most intelligent person in the world.

You might think that sounds like hyperbole. It's not.

Akshay Venkatesh recently won the Fields Medal, which is often referred to as the Nobel Prize of maths. This puts him in rarefied air – the medal is awarded to only four people in the world, once every four years.

When I heard the news of this remarkable achievement, my immediate response was: "well of course he did". Because Akshay was no average kid, to put it ridiculously mildly.

In fact, when I say I went to school with him, that's a little misleading. I was indeed in a class with Akshay – it's just that he happened to be 7 years younger than me at the time.

You see, when Akshay was just 10 years old, he would walk up from the primary school campus to join our final-year calculus class. Around the same time, he was studying university-level physics.

He began university in earnest at the age of 13 – the same year that his chronological peers started high school. He graduated with a bachelor's degree at 16, had a PhD at 20, and was a mathematics professor at 26.

Suffice it to say, he is hardwired differently from the rest of us. Even when he was a kid half our size, it was obvious to everyone that we were in the presence of a world-class mind.

Since Akshay won the Fields Medal, I've read a few articles about his work. It's really quite straightforward – he has synthesised analytic number theory, homogeneous dynamics, topology and representation theory, which has resolved longstanding problems in areas such as the equidistribution of arithmetic objects.

You'll probably be relieved to hear that this work is understandable to only a handful of people in the world. It is to the average person what psychoanalytic theory is to the average mollusc.

So I think it's fair to say that most of us have the square root of bugger-all to learn from the work itself. But what I did find interesting was this description from a Business Standard article:

"Maths encompasses a wide variety of sub-disciplines, and few mathematicians are experts at more than one or two areas. Venkatesh, however, has always been an avid reader, delving into entirely different areas of mathematics purely for entertainment."

Now, you might find it difficult to relate to the idea of reading mathematics "purely for entertainment", but the broader principle is something we can all learn from.

Hear me out.

Apparently Akshay uses his diverse interests to "swiftly develop insights that can be applied to other branches of maths". Where others have become stuck in a certain way of thinking about a problem, he introduces a completely leftfield perspective.

This would appear to be a good example of what is known as the Medici effect. Coined by the entrepreneur Frans Johannson, this term refers to the innovation that happens when disciplines intersect, such that ideas from one field are brought into another.

While most of us won't ever make the kind of groundbreaking discoveries described by the Medici effect, there is a valuable lesson here.

Namely, curiosity is a catalyst for creativity.

This is why it's so important for us to take an interest in the world beyond our own industry. Many people in advertising will tell you that they get their ideas from all sorts of seemingly unrelated places – books, films, art, history, people-watching, perhaps even maths. Without this broader perspective, the work turns in on itself and inevitably becomes conventional.

So you don't need to be a genius to see things that others haven't. Sometimes you just need to open your eyes – and your mind – to what else is out there.

AGENC
FESTIV
DEADLINE CM
DESIGN BY COMMITTEE   CHAN
AWARD BAIT   LOREM IPSUM   P
FUCK THIS I'M AN ARTIST   F
TV IS DEAD   MUM DOESN'T K
FAILED CAMPAIGN   5TH ROUN
TICKETS NOW AVAILABLE A

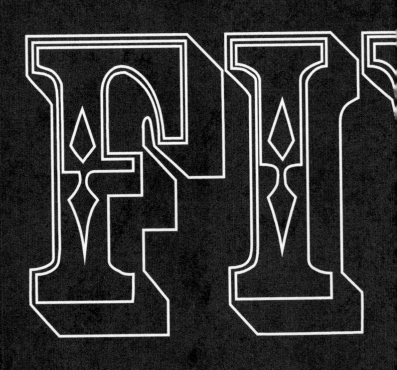

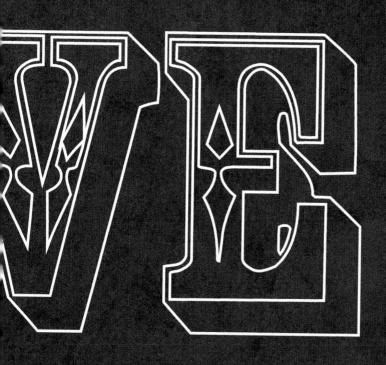

BUSINESS

BUSINESS TERMS AND WHAT THEY REALLY MEAN

Rockstar	Boring guy in a suit.
Rainmaker	Boring guy in a suit who has loud phone conversations about 'deals'.
Consultant	Boring guy in a suit who draws incomprehensible shapes on whiteboards.
Stakeholder	Someone who must be engaged.
Engaged	Something that a stakeholder must be.
Nimble	Unable to commit to a plan.
Iterative	A process that takes longer but also achieves a worse result.
Blockchain	I have absolutely no idea, but everything must be on it, or in it, or something.

THE PRETENSION TRAP: WHY BUZZWORDS ARE HURTING YOUR BUSINESS

I RECENTLY PERUSED THE WEBSITES OF SOME CONSULTING COMPANIES, IN AN ATTEMPT TO UNDERSTAND HOW THEY DIFFERENTIATE THEMSELVES. ALAS, I REMAIN NONE THE WISER.

All of these companies used every one of the following terms to describe themselves and their services:

- Innovative
- Value-adding
- Quality
- Passionate
- Committed
- Empowering
- Engaged.

In some cases, several of these adjectives (assuming we accept the use of 'quality' as an adjective, which I don't) were used in combination. Take this little mash-up of banalities, for example:

"... innovative and committed to delivering value-adding ideas, products and services".

And the kicker? Each of these companies – demonstrating an admittedly admirable degree of chutzpah – described its offering as 'unique'.

Never mind that this kind of linguistic guff leaves most people cold. The bigger problem it creates for these companies is that all of their major competitors are saying exactly the same things as they are. If any of them do in fact have a significant point of difference, then they certainly don't communicate it.

So why do they do it?

Probably because they think it sounds impressive. But that puts them in an awkward place. And since we're talking about the consulting industry, perhaps the best way to explain this is with a 2 x 2 matrix.

THE COMMUNICATIONS INTELLIGENCE MATRIX

	Trying to sound intelligent	Not trying to sound intelligent
Intelligent	Literature and stuff	Charlie and the Chocolate Factory
Not Intelligent	Corporate buzzwords	Magazines with titles ending in an exclamation mark

We might call the lower-left cell of this matrix the 'pretension trap'. It's a trap, for businesses, because it means they sound just like everyone else – a potentially fatal mistake in a competitive market.

The pretension trap is a marketer's dream

If you're in the corporate world, this state of affairs represents a golden opportunity. When all your competitors sound the same, eschewing the 'accepted' language of business communications represents a ridiculously easy way to differentiate your brand. Can you say that about any other aspect of your business?

Not only that, but you'll actually sound more intelligent, as shown by a cognitive study with the wonderful title 'Consequences of Erudite Vernacular Utilized Irrespective of Necessity: Problems with Using Long Words Needlessly':

"... write clearly and simply if you can, and you'll be more likely to be thought of as intelligent".

Time to get smart?

THE CEO'S PRAYER

Our Boss, who art in the
penthouse office,
Hallowed be thy acronym.
Thy vision embedded,
Thy strategy be actioned
going forward,
On Earth as it is on the 58th
floor overlooking the bay.
Give us this day our 1/330th
of your daily bread,
And forgive us our unmet KPIs,
As we forgive those whose
own unmet KPIs jeopardise
our modest livelihoods.
And lead us not into mergers,
But deliver us from team-building.
For thine is the Company,
The political influence,
and the Bentley,
For an average of 4.4 years.
A man (usually).

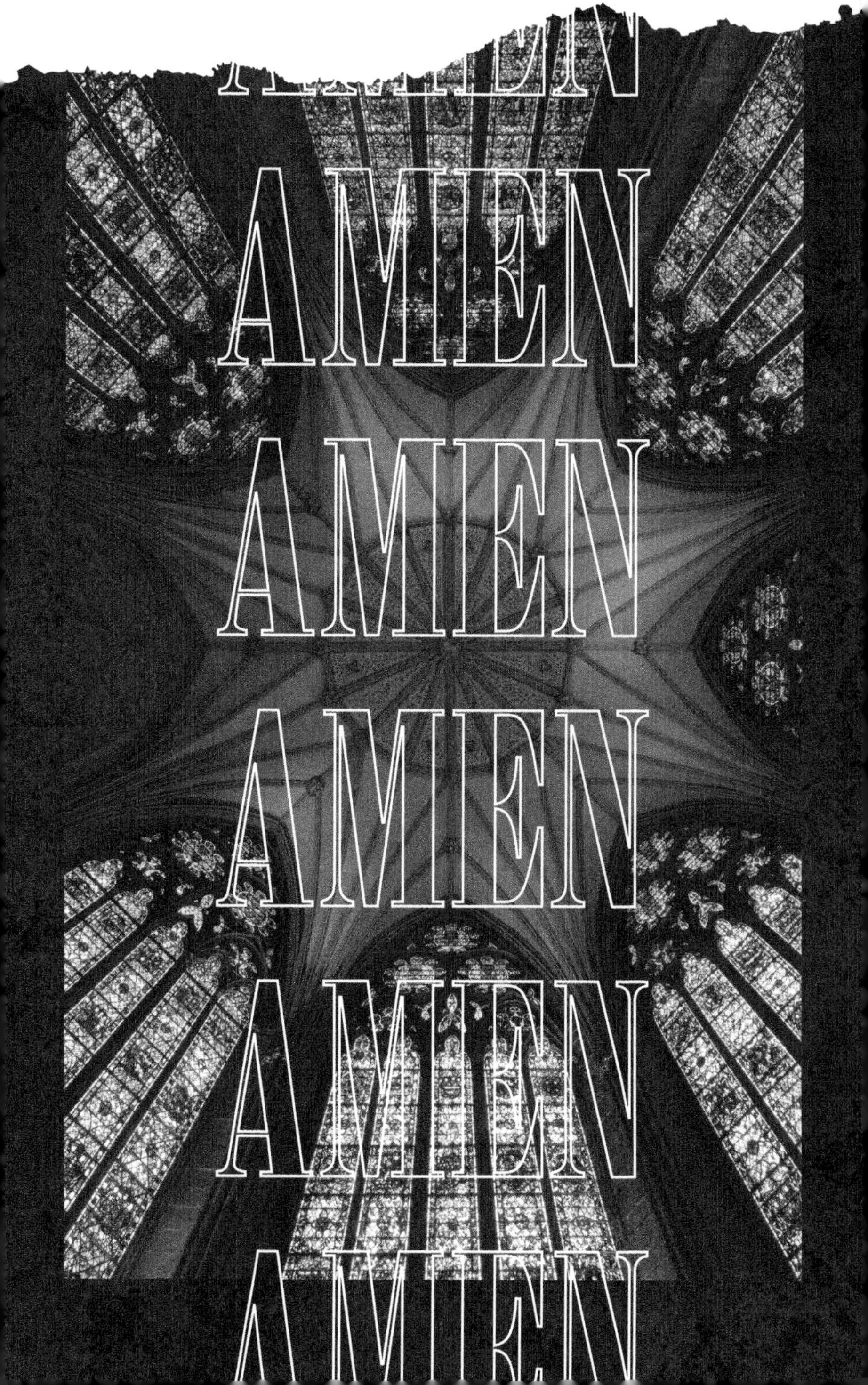
AMEN
AMEN
AMEN
AMEN

HOW TO WRITE A CONSULTING FIRM REPORT

1. The tone you should aim for is 'godlike condescension'.

2. Do not, under any circumstances, look up the meaning of the Dunning-Kruger effect.

3. Start with a statement of the glaringly obvious yet ridiculously vague. Something like: '2020 will present challenges for business'.

4. Stuff as many buzzwords as possible into the report. The buzzier the better.

5. Don't just settle for existing buzzwords. Invent some new ones exclusively for the report.

6. Just when you think it can't get any more incomprehensible, add a few more.

7. Never use a short word where a long one will do.

8. Leave no noun un-verbed.

9. Read the report to your mother. If she recognises it as the English language, rewrite it.

10. Charge a ball-tearingly large amount of money for it. And don't worry – the people who pay for this kind of report don't care whether it's any good.

WHAT HAPPENED ONLINE IN THE PAST 60 SECONDS

60

7 million digital ads not seen by a single human

1.5 million self-aggrandising LinkedIn posts

450,000 misconstrued tweets

4 million profoundly embarrassing Google queries

250 bible orders activated by Alexa during intimate moments

300 million unread 'reply all' emails

6.5 million private Facebook posts scoured for personal data

200,000 awkward Tinder dates

People often ask me how I became a LinkedIn rockstar.

That's a tough question. It's like asking Pavarotti how he became a great singer.

But I have to answer it, because these no-names deserve a response from their idol.

What I tell them is what I'm going to tell you now – for FREE. I'm generous like that, which is one of the things I love about me.

My success is made up of 50% genius and 50% humility. Plus 20% rule-breaking.

Every day I wake up at 3am, which is half an hour after I go to bed, and scream "I'M CRUSHING TODAY".

Then I start thought leading. I make a point of leading at least ten thoughts before getting out of bed.

For breakfast, I snort three raw eggs blended with the tears of my competitors.

And that's when the hustling starts.

I hustle 26 hours a day. Some people say "Ryan, that's impossible", but that's because they're not trying hard enough. I disrupt the space-time continuum every. Freaking. Day. Only losers obey the laws of physics.

Of course, to hustle as hard as I do, I need to be in peak physical condition.

So I run constantly, even when I'm sleeping. I run the equivalent of four marathons every day. I could be the marathon world champion, in fact, but I'm too busy influencing the hell out of people and generally smashing it in the business world.

When I go to the gym, it's me versus the equipment. I don't stop until one of us breaks, which is why I've already destroyed six treadmills this week. LOSERS.

All of this boils down to my formula for life. Great mind + incredible body = winningness to the power of awesome.

So now you know the secrets of my stardom. You're welcome.

DESCRIBE YOURSELF AS A THOUGHT LEADER

YOU ARE NOW A THOUGHT LEADER

A SIMPLE GUIDE TO LAUNCHING YOUR OWN STARTUP

Think of a problem that, if solved, would significantly improve people's quality of life and make a meaningful contribution to social progress.

Now ignore that problem. Instead, think of a different problem that already has a perfectly good solution – say, tooth brushing.

Come up with an alternative solution to this problem, involving a complex combination of trendy and totally unnecessary technology. For example, you could create an app that allowed people to voice-activate the delivery of a 3D-printed toothbrush to their house by drone.

Give your startup a cool name by thinking of a suitably descriptive word and then removing one vowel from it. In this case, Brushr or Dentl would be perfect.

Now you will need to attract some investors. The best way to do this is to mention that your idea involves the use of blockchain, irrespective of whether this is true. And don't worry if you have absolutely no idea what blockchain is – neither do they.

Enter your startup for an advertising award. Since it clearly has nothing to do with advertising, it's sure to do well.

When your startup is found to be engaging in unscrupulous practices – which it undoubtedly will – just explain that you are 'disrupting' the traditional notions of ethics and morality.

I WAS AT A BAR, MINDING MY OWN BUSINESS. I WAS JUST SITTING THERE IN MY TAILORED SUIT, QUIETLY SIPPING A GLASS OF 1961 GRANGE HERMITAGE, BECAUSE IT WAS A TUESDAY. OUT OF THE CORNER OF MY EYE, I SAW THEM APPROACHING. FOOTBALL HOOLIGANS. FIFTY OF THEM. THEY OBVIOUSLY THOUGHT I WAS AN EASY TARGET. IT REMINDED ME OF ALL THE OTHER PEOPLE WHO HAVE UNDERESTIMATED ME SINCE I WAS BORN IN A SIBERIAN WASTELAND AND RAISED BY WOLVES. BY THE TIME THE FIRST ONE LUNGED AT ME, I'D KNOCKED OUT 20 OF THEM COLD WITH THE POWER OF MY INTELLECT ALONE. THE REST OF THEM BEGGED FOR MERCY, JUST LIKE THE WEAKLINGS I DESTROY EVERY DAY IN THE BOARDROOM. "AS YOU WERE, GENTLEMEN," I SAID, AND STROLLED TO THE EXIT. JUST THEN, A 2 YEAR-OLD CHILD STOPPED ME AND SAID "MISTER, I ASPIRE TO EMULATE YOUR GREATNESS. YOU'RE A FORMIDABLE OPPONENT BUT YOU ALSO EXUDE CLASS". SMART KID. MORAL OF THE STORY: BITCOIN.

I HAVE A SIMPLE TACTIC WHEN INTERVIEWING PEOPLE FOR A JOB. I CALL IT THE 'LOSER TEST'.

When the interviewee walks into the room, I offer them a choice of three chairs. If they choose the middle one, I terminate the interview immediately. There's no way I'm working with any middle-chair motherfuckers.

Then I ask them a series of basic questions about the architectural characteristics of ancient Mesoamerican civilisations.

If they get any of these wrong, I think to myself: what else are they going to get wrong in a fast-paced office environment?

So I send those duds packing too. Usually in tears, which simply confirms to me that they never would have cut it. It's heartening to know that I've made the right decision.

Next, I give them a military code to break.

That always weeds out a few idiots.

And finally, I ask them to tell me exactly what I'm thinking at that specific point in time. You'd be amazed how many people get this wrong.

So that's my recruitment secret. In the end, it's all about hiring people who want to be part of an inclusive culture.

Everyone else can fuck off.

A BEGINNER'S GUIDE TO LINKEDIN

in structions
in structions
in structions
in structions
in structions
in structions
in struction
in struction
in struction

1. The first rule is that you must post a longwinded, self-congratulatory description of your 'journey' to ostentatious wealth. Don't worry if it seems like an impossible exaggeration – that means you're doing it right.

2. If you can't think of anything original to say, just copy-and-paste someone else's post and claim it as your own. Attribution is for losers.

3.Use.

This.

Format.

4. Make a wildly uninformed pronouncement that such-and-such is dead and bling-blong is the future.

5. Confidently explain the secrets that have made a particular company successful, despite having absolutely no way of knowing those secrets.

6. Describe what we can all learn from [insert trivial event with no educational value].

7. If you are going to share posts by influencers (which you absolutely must), be sure to add your own insightful comment such as 'This' or 'True!'.

8. Do not concern yourself with correct spelling, grammar or punctuation. The '24/7 hustlers' of LinkedIn abhor such pedantry.

9. If you find that there isn't enough emotionally incontinent attention-seeking on here for you, try Facebook.

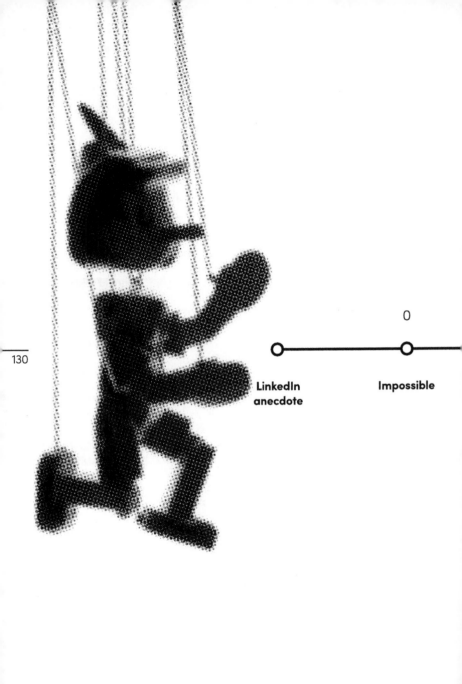

0

LinkedIn
anecdote

Impossible

PROBABILITY SCALE

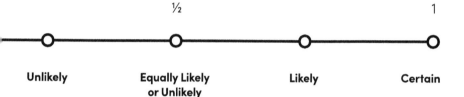

$\frac{1}{2}$ 1

Unlikely   **Equally Likely**   **Likely**   **Certain**
            or Unlikely

WORDS

NEVER

NEVER

NEVER

THINGS
YOU SHOULD
NEVER
SAY TO A
COPYWRITER

There is no brief for this job, as such.

I'd write it myself but I don't have time.

Make it punchy.

It just needs wordsmithing.

Our audience is professional so please use more buzzwords.

Nobody reads long copy anymore.

What about "delivering innovative solutions"?

This online banner ad will make or break the campaign. By the way, the word limit is 7.

You can't start a sentence with "And".

Our tracked changes are attached.

We've shown it to everyone in the company for their thoughts. Bill from Accounts didn't like the tone and Tommy the office beagle pissed on it.

THE
COPYWRITER'S
DICTIONARY

Agnosticopy
Copy that fails to make the reader believe.

Carbon copy
Copy that bears a striking similarity to that of a competitor.

Colonoscopy
1. An over-punctuated piece of copy.

2. Copy that is firmly up its own behind.

Coppee
Copywriter-strength coffee. As in: "I probably shouldn't have had two coppees; I think I can see through time".

Coptical illusion
Copy so badly kerned that it appears to have a different meaning from that which was intended.

Copycat killer
A copywriter who puts an abrupt end to any request for a cat-related social media campaign.

Copy-out
Use of a copywriting cliché. As in: "I can't believe this company describes itself as 'innovative' – what a copy-out".

Copyrolalia
Copy characterised by vulgar or scatological references.

Copyromania
A compulsive preference for copy that states the flaming obvious. Highly prevalent in the automotive industry.

Copyrrhic victory
The result of sabotaging copy to thwart someone else's achievement. As in: "I wasn't prepared to let my art director get his way, so I had to opt for a copyrrhic victory".

Lambruscopy
Copy written after consuming a cheap bottle of wine. Appears to be extraordinarily clever and witty at the time of writing but induces a sense of shame the following day.

Molluscopy
Copy so unremarkable that it gets mistaken for the slug on a print proof.

Obfuscopy
Jargon-riddled copy intended to make the reader think "this company is too smart to bother with making this comprehensible".

Orinocopy
Copy based on an obscure 1980s pop-culture reference, which therefore appeals only to the writer's generation.

Osso buccopy
Copy that's delicious, on the proviso that you don't look at it too closely.

Talcopy
Extremely dry copy that sucks all the interest out of a piece of communication. Often related to insurance products.

[MATHS CLASS]

Teacher: To specify a point on the graph, we start with x.

Simon Sinek raises hand

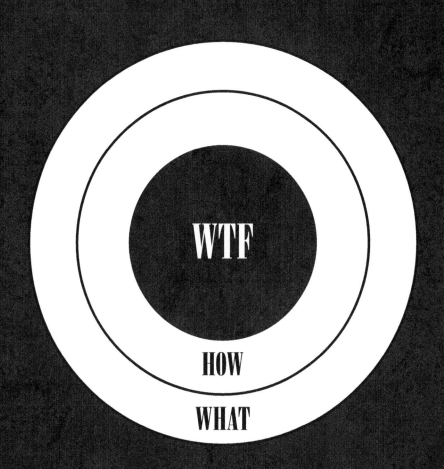

THE TEMPLATE FOR MODERN PRINT ADS

VISUAL PUN

LOGO
COPY (OPTIONAL)

IF CLASSIC

TAGLINES

WERE

REWRITTEN

TODAY

IF CLASSIC TAGLINES
WERE REWRITTEN TODAY

We try harder — **Driving ambition**

Don't leave home without it — **Live convenient**

It does exactly what
it says on the tin — **Delivering on expectations**

Never knowingly undersold — **Passionate about value**

Coke is it — **Experience the it**

Got milk? — **Pasteurisation for your utilisation**

Just do it — **Innovative doing solutions**

Beanz meanz Heinz — **Beanfulness. Redefined.**

ANY TAGLINE YOU WANT SO LONG AS IT'S RIDICULOUS

TAGLINES.
WHAT TO THINK OF THEM?
WHEN IT COMES TO TAGLINES
FOR CAR BRANDS, WHAT I
USUALLY THINK OF THEM IS:
"NOTHING COULD MAKE ME
WANT THAT CAR LESS".
CONSIDER, FOR EXAMPLE,
THESE THREE LEMONS.

'Innovation that excites'

Using the word 'innovation' is the copywriting equivalent of talking about the weather – assuming you talk about the weather using hackneyed corporate jargon. So this tagline is not off to a good start.

Whichever committee wrote this (and you just know it was a committee) perhaps realised that innovation alone would not be enough to get people, well, excited. So no doubt some amateur psychologist hit on the brilliant idea of "injecting an emotional dimension" by adding copy that excites. This was taken literally, of course, because committees do not deal in metaphor.

Taken as a whole, this line is beyond ludicrous. Customers are not excited by innovation. They might be excited by what this car can do for them, like elevate their social status or, God forbid, get them from A to B. But no such benefit can be gleaned from this copy.

'I think therefore I Amarok'

I understand what they're trying to do here. I get it – in the same way I would 'get' sausages by seeing what they are made from.

It's not a bad idea to include the brand name in a tagline or campaign, by any means; it can be very effective because it provides customers with a mnemonic. The 'Ariston and On and On' slogan is often cited as a successful example of this technique. But there was a point to that line. It specifically communicated the benefit of a brand of kitchen appliances (namely, not having to replace the damn things all the time).

But what, pray tell, does this car have to do with Descartes' meditations on the nature of existence? Perhaps it's that we only really know we are alive because a dream would never present us with anything this silly. Honestly, 'I Amarok'? That's the kind of wordplay you might expect from a work experience kid. If you ask me, this tagline is copywriting contrivance at its worst. Actually, make that second worst, because then there's this...

'The romance of performance'

If you're looking for the gold standard of awful taglines, here it is in all its ostentatious, unadulterated glory.

This is my hypothesis for how it came about.

The agency responsible for it had an 'email malfunction', and inadvertently sent this option to the client, when in fact it had been the intended tagline for a different product (a treatment for erectile dysfunction).

Unexpectedly, the client loved it. They felt that this line perfectly encapsulated their brand strategy, since it was underpinned by an appeal to the emotion of female buyers (or, as they put it, 'buyer personas') but also tapped into the company's vision for 'optimal performance'.

Suffice it to say that if they were going for romance, all they achieved was turgidity.

THE 20 MOST IMPORTANT ROLES IN ADVERTISING

Digital Director

Innovation Director

Strategy Director

Digital Innovation Strategist

Digital Strategy Innovator

Someone Who Used To Be In
Advertising But Now Just Moralises
About Trendy Political Issues

Snapchat Specialist

Millennial Whisperer

Media Fraud Conspirator

New Technology Hyperbolist

Buzzword Barista

UI Designer

UX Designer

CX Designer

All Other Designers Of
Two-Letter Acronyms

Work Experience Kid

Chatbot

Creative Director

Art Director

Copywriter

ON THE FRONT LINE AGAINST THE JARGONAUTS

I think I speak for many copywriters when I say that it sometimes feels as if we're losing the war of words.

(Sorry for starting on a bit of a downer, but that's kind of my thing.)

Long-copy ads are rare these days. Cheap 'content' is everywhere. And don't get me started on f😡😡😡ing emojis.

But these are trifling matters, relatively speaking. I think the biggest enemy of our trade – and those of you who know me even slightly won't be surprised to hear this – is corporate jargon.

Or 'bollocks', to use my preferred term for it.

Yes, yes, I know, this is a topic that's been done to death, so I won't bore/infuriate you with another list of excruciating buzzwords. But the fact is: this problem is not going away.

If anything, corpspeak is becoming ever more pervasive. It's spreading and metastasising like some colourless, soporific tumour.

Once the preserve of management theorists – bless their possibly robotic hearts – corporate jargon is now undeniably mainstream.

To wit, sportspeople now routinely talk about streamlining processes and meeting KPIs and managing controllables.

So I think it's fair to say that we're at the far right

Fair enough. But you and I know that corporate jargon is not (just) a silly source of amusement. It corrupts communication and it inhibits clear thinking.

This point was made recently by the wonderful Australian author, speechwriter and gobbledygook-slayer, Don Watson, who wrote:

'One can't think in the fog that management

But obfuscation is only part of the problem. The worst aspect of corporate jargon, I think, is its dehumanising effect. For evidence, look no further than the fact that, in the parlance of modern business, people are not even people. They are 'resources' or 'talent' or (ugh) 'capital'.

And this gets to the nub of the problem for you and me. Because fundamentally, copywriting relies on understanding people and using language that connects with people.

THE BUZZWORD ADOPTION CURVE

Politicians

Middle managers

Footballers

CEOs

People in productive jobs

INNOVATORS EARLY ADOPTERS EARLY MAJORITY LATE MAJORITY LAGGARDS

of the buzzword adoption curve.

For many people, the response to all this is: so what?

'Ryan,' they probably think to themselves after my fifth unhinged rant of the day, 'give it a rest, will you? Does it really matter if people want to sound like pseudo-intellectual drones?'

jargon deliberately creates. One can't know in it. Politics needs thought and language equally. Civil society does.'

We've all experienced the fog that he refers to. You need only read a big company's website or a CEO's memo to appreciate the obfuscatory nature of this kind of language.

At the risk of stating the bleeding obvious, David Ogilvy knew this. Which is why he described jargon words as the 'hallmarks of a pretentious ass'. (Tell us what you really think, David.)

So I believe that copywriters have an important role in fighting the scourge of corporate jargon.

Onwards, copy soldiers.

This article was originally published on the ProCopywriters website.

MEDICAL CERTIFICATE

Could you jazz up the title?
Every doctor uses this.

I don't like the use of 'whom'.
Too old-fashioned.

TO WHOM IT MAY CONCERN,

I CERTIFY THAT I HAVE EXAMINED JOHN AND THAT HE WILL BE UNFIT FOR HIS USUAL WORK DUTIES FOR A PERIOD OF 2 WEEKS, AS HE IS CURRENTLY UNWELL WITH BRONCHITIS.

'Unfit' sounds very negative. Please change to 'momentarily fitness-challenged'.

Are you sure about this diagnosis?
My nephew did a biology unit at school and he disagrees with it.

REGARDS,

DR JONES

**IS YOUR PRODUCT
INNOVATIVE?**

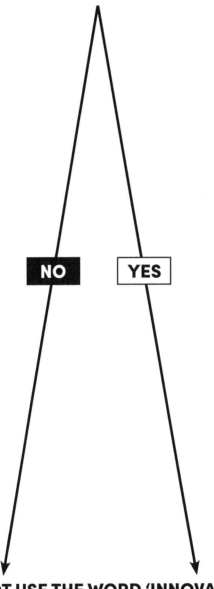

NO   **YES**

DO NOT USE THE WORD 'INNOVATIVE'

WHAT KIND OF WRITER ARE YOU?

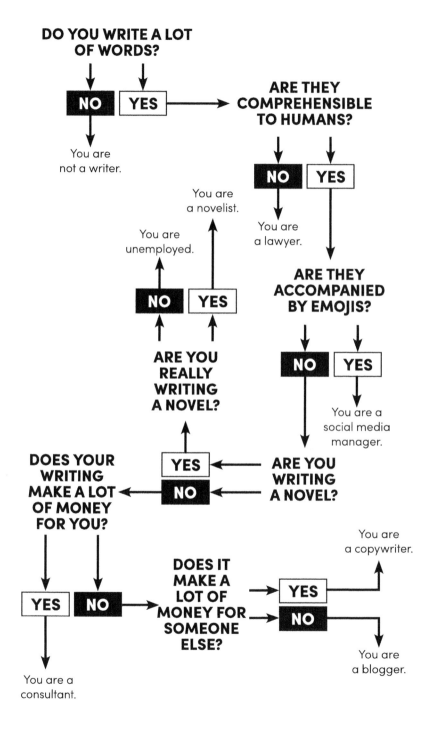

IF ENGINEERING WAS LIKE COPYWRITING...

*BRIDGEC

"Move those girders."

"But the bridge will collapse."

"Just do it."

OLLAPSES*

"We're very disappointed that the bridge collapsed. We don't think we should pay for a completed bridge."

"Our CEO's son has just done a week of work experience at an engineering firm. He's got some ideas for a replacement bridge."

"We've decided to crowd-source ideas for the bridge. We can get 50 bridges for your price."

"Is this bridge built for inbound traffic? I went to a conference last week that said outbound is dead."

"We really like the Golden Gate Bridge. That's the kind of bridge we're looking for. Budget is $500."

CHAPTER

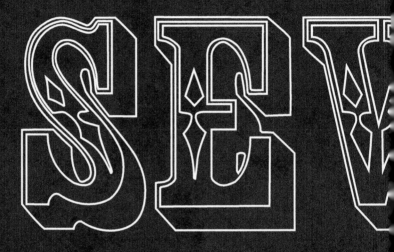

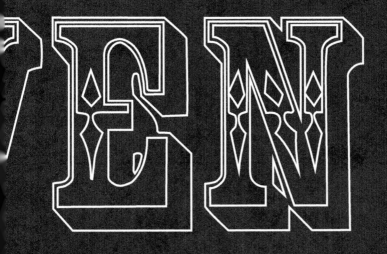

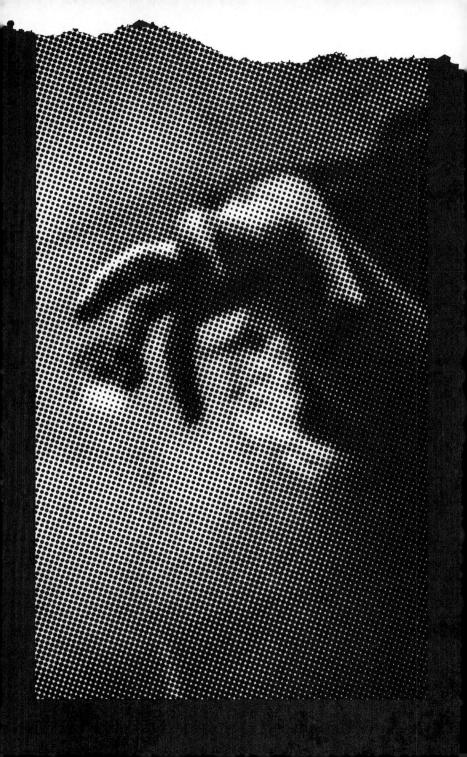

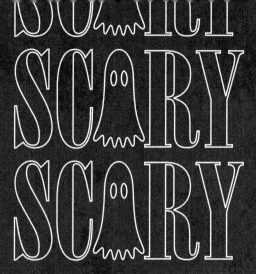

SCARY
SCARY
SCARY

THE SCARIEST PHRASES
IN MARKETING

What's our
brand purpose?

We need to be
on TikTok.

Let's take an
agile approach.

Gary V said...

We know that modern
consumers have the
attention span of
a goldfish.

Millennials crave
experiences.

Millennials only buy
from companies that
share their values.

[Any other comment
about millennials]

What's our influencer
strategy?

[Literally anything]
is dead.

DEAR BOBBY

...ely, I ...eliver

before any elves get paid. Let me tell you, there are some angry little bastards in my workshop. The "sharing economy", my ample arse.

Honestly, you should hear what these Santr blokes are saying. According to their CEO, "the Santr brand embodies the true spirit of giving". What a load of ho ho horseshit. Those Silicon Valley motherfuckers – don't repeat that word, Bobby – wouldn't know the true spirit of

giving if it smacked them in their smug faces. And as for those "beards" of theirs: bitches, please. I've been growing this bad boy for 250 years.

I'm sure you'll get your toys this year, Bobby. But you tell your mummy and daddy that if they get stung by surge pricing for the delivery, well, that would be a real shame.

Welcome to the new world order, son. It sucks baubles.

Santa

PROJECT BRIEF

Client: S. Claus

Job name: Global
Christmas gift initiative

Product: Augmented recreation
devices (formerly known as 'toys')

TARGET AUDIENCE
Juvenilennials
(formerly known as 'kids').

OBJECTIVE
To elevate the role of elf-
manufactured augmented
recreation devices from functional
items to engaging interactive
experiences that empower
juvenilennials to self-actualise
their creative potential.

DISTRIBUTION CHANNELS
Our research indicates that
juvenilennials are increasingly
sceptical of traditional sleigh-
based distribution, due to
negative word-of-mouth from
key influencers (specifically, older
siblings). Therefore, this year's
campaign must incorporate
digital alternatives such as VR
(virtual reindeer), Ubereindeer
and AmazOn Dasher.

TAGLINE
Innovative festive
solutions. Delivered.

AMAZON ACQUIRES SANTA CLAUS & CO

NORTH POLE, 6 DECEMBER 2018

Stocking markets reacted strongly today after Amazon announced its acquisition of the non-profit children's toy company, Santa Claus & Co.

An Amazon spokesperson said the decision to acquire Santa Claus & Co was driven by Amazon's commitment to offering a full-spectrum, end-to-end Christmas solution.

"There are obvious synergies between our organisations.

Santa is an iconic brand with a global hoofprint that will help us optimise our seasonal gifting services. And we're particularly excited about the fact that Santa's elves work tirelessly without remuneration – this is very much aligned with our approach to labour efficiency."

The acquisition will have significant structural implications for Santa & Co. The company has been based in the Arctic since its inception, but Amazon is rumoured to be seeking colossal bids for a second headquarters, to be known as HoQ2. Meanwhile, Santa's traditional delivery system is set to be replaced by reindrones.

Santa himself will step down from his role after several hundred years of service. He will be subject to a non-compete Claus.

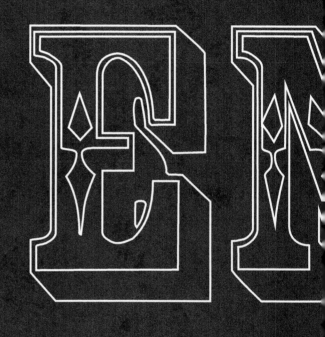

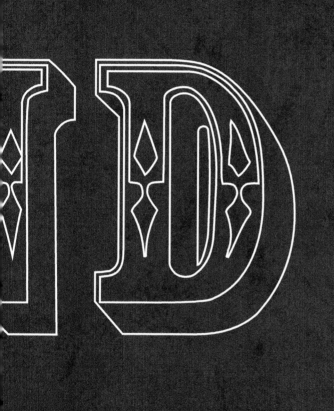

Printed in Great Britain
by Amazon

34622905R00098